HOW TO WIN IN THE
CHESS ENDINGS

Also by I. A. Horowitz

HOW TO WIN IN THE CHESS OPENINGS

MODERN IDEAS IN THE CHESS OPENINGS

HOW TO WIN IN THE MIDDLE GAME OF CHESS

How to Win

IN THE

CHESS ENDINGS

BY

I. A. Horowitz

With 171 diagrams

DAVID McKAY COMPANY, INC.

NEW YORK

For Edna

Contents

Foreword

I HAVE been prompted to write this book for a number of reasons. To begin with, while I do not subscribe to the proposition that when you say "A" you must also say "B," I am, nevertheless, impelled to complete my works on the opening and middle game with one on the end game.

Be that as it may, there were even more compelling reasons. While there are some books on the ending currently on the market, and particularly a very fine production in *Basic Chess Endings,* not a single one caters to any extent to the learner who requires step-by-step explanations of what it is all about. *How to Win in the Chess Endings,* while not ambitious in scope, on the contrary, painstakingly covers the pertinent details.

In a sense, it is a paradox that this book should come out last. All tutors agree that the logical presentation of the game of chess should begin with the endings; that it is easier to comprehend the movements of two units rather than thirty-two. The demand for opening- and middle-game information, however, was a deciding factor.

One thing is certain! If a learner knows the endings, he not only will get a finer feel for the other departments, he is sure to reach a happy ending.

I. A. HOROWITZ

HOW TO WIN IN THE
CHESS ENDINGS

1

Why the End Game?

THE GAME OF CHESS is divided into three parts—the opening, the middle game, and the end game. Because the flow of ideas begins in the opening, courses through the middle game, and winds up in the end game, it may seem that the study of chess should pursue the same sequence. Curiously, and precisely, it should not.

In the beginning, to be sure, there are thirty-two units on the chessboard. It is only reasonable to assume, however, that a player who cannot manage two or three units correctly is at a complete loss when confronted with thirty-two. Hence, it is easy to see the need for learning the powers and properties of the single units in relation to each other before embracing the combined, progressive potentiality of the many.

The end game, moreover, contains basic positions akin to the axioms of mathematics. To know these positions is to acquire a storehouse of fundamentals which are part and parcel of nearly every game. This knowledge is really the solid groundwork of foresight, the prime requisite of planning.

Foresight in the opening, for example, is nothing more than a predisposed knowledge of the middle game, and possibly the end game. Foresight in the middle game is knowledge of the end game. Foresight is the essential attribute for favorably projecting the future.

To crystallize the thought, let us assume one of the usual variety of middle-game positions. In it we find innumerable continuations, many alternate choices. To attack, to defend, to stall, to swap: these are vexing problems. If one could foresee with certainty a favorable result by one of these actions, he would know what to do. There would be no problem.

Rarely, however, is the issue so cut and dried. Almost always there is present an element of speculation. Yet it goes without saying that a favorable result brought about with a minimum of risk is the correct procedure. And here is where knowledge of the end game is the answer. Because the end game has so few units, it is often possible to calculate its consequences without fear of contradiction—without risk. Thus the first course of action to be considered is that which leads to an end game.

Even so we need *knowledge* of the end game. It is one thing to be able to handle a winning end game when placed actually in it. It is quite another thing, starting from our middle-game position, to be able to judge if the end game will be a favorable one. Rare is the talent that can run out mentally the moves which bring about the end game and then superimpose another mental reckoning of whether or not that position is a winning one. Our essential foresight in the middle game must then include a sure knowledge of what end-game positions are winning ones.

Now that we have established the need for learning the end game, let us proceed to the task.

KING VERSUS PAWN

When a Pawn reaches the eighth rank, it is a well-known fact that it will promote to a piece of its own color, most likely a Queen. This power to expand is one of the most decisive factors of the entire game. That is why it is necessary in the end game to watch every enemy Pawn advance with surreptitious caution.

Because the general run of end games is garnished with a lot of material and because even one puny move may affect the final result, the calculations are generally deep, profound, and exacting. It is rather a tedious procedure, in any given position, to count the number of moves it requires for a Pawn to Queen in order to determine whether the Pawn can be stopped by the opposing King. It is even more tedious mentally to observe: "I go here; he goes there; I go here; he goes there, etc." The chance of error or of a miscount is too great. Considering, moreover, that the calculation usually comes at the tail end of other maneuvers not yet made but only in the imagination, the total number of moves to be observed are many—often too many for the average chess player. Under the circumstances, a short cut is desirable to avert tortuous analysis. Fortunately, for one type of position, there is such a device. There is an easy way of calculating the relationship of a King to an enemy Pawn so that you can determine with exactitude whether or not the Pawn may be stopped.

With White on the move in this position, can the Black Pawn be prevented from queening?

In order to make the calculations step by step, we observe the following moves:

1	K-B6	P-R4
2	K-Q5	P-R5
3	K-K4	P-R6
4	K-B3	P-R7
5	K-N2	....

The Pawn queens—to no avail!

The Pawn can be stopped. But we have been taxed with calculating five accurate moves. Since the diagrammed position may be part of earlier calculations still in the mind of the player, we note the player is compelled to look ahead for a number of moves, possibly beyond his ken. There is a much more simple way of doing the same thing.

Here is the very same position. Only this time we have used a device for determining whether the Pawn can be stopped. We draw a line on the diagonal of the Pawn, extending from Black's KR3 to QB8. Then we extend the line straight upward to the same rank on which the Black Pawn stands. We have described a triangle. Now we describe a second triangle from Black's KR3 to KR8 to QB8 and back to KR3. Together, these triangles form a square. If the White King can enter the square, the Pawn can be stopped.

At first sight all of this effort appears to be greater than the

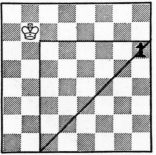

troublesome calculations above. After a while, however, the eye can be trained to envisage the square of the Pawn at a glance, and the calculations will be made in a split second.

Here Are a Few More Examples:

 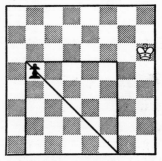

With White on the move, can the Pawn be stopped?

No. The White King is out of the square.

What is the square of the Black Pawn?

The Black Pawn forms two squares, one on its right and one on its left. Parts of the square, in this case, are actually imaginary since they extend beyond the scope of the board. If the White King can get into any square within the square of the Pawn, the King will stop the Pawn.

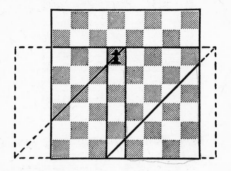

Exception to the Rule

Can the White King stop the Black Pawn?

When a Pawn is on the second rank, its advance of two squares on the first move must be taken into account. Hence, for the purposes of quick calculation, the Pawn must be considered as on the third rank. In this position, the White King cannot stop the Pawn, appearances to the contrary notwithstanding.

We may represent the "Pawn square" diagrammatically in this wise:

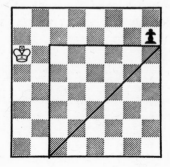

HOW TO STUDY THE END GAME

Rarely will an exact book position occur in a game. The positions that will occur, however, may embody the self-same principles as the book position. In order to make assurance doubly sure that you understand the principle rather than the given diagrammed position, set up your own exercises. Compose positions similar to the ones you are studying and ask yourself what difference, if any, exists between the given position and the ones you have composed. You will be surprised at the answers and your knowledge and proficiency at handling end games will increase immeasurably.

2

The Power of the King

SOME GAMES OF CHESS never leave the opening: the "brilliancy" is short and sweet. Between players of approximately equal strength, however, a game is more than likely to reach an ending. And it is in the ending that the game is won, lost, or drawn.

The story is told about two beginners, completely ignorant of the primary end-game concepts, continuing play in an end game featuring Kings—and nothing else! A master watched the absurd struggle for some time but finally gave up waiting for them to abandon it. When he returned later and asked if they had agreed to a draw, one of the beginners replied: "No—he mated me."

This incident is hardly typical of chess players, even beginners. Yet it is surprising to learn how little some nonbeginners know about such really basic positions as even King and Pawn end games.

In King and Pawn endings, the position of the Kings is often the decisive factor. King and Pawn versus King and Pawn may be a win or a draw, depending on how far advanced the Pawns may be, on whether one or both Pawns can be stopped from queening, or on whether one King can force the other King out of the way, or in end-game terminology, "gaining the opposition," and so gobble up the enemy Pawn.

Often one King is able in a materially even position to reach and capture the opponent's Pawns, while the opposing King cannot. The "King position" is thus a simple demonstration of a "positional" advantage being converted into a "material" one.

Let us now turn to a study of the movement of the King in King and Pawn end games.

REACHING A FIXED GOAL

After you have become familiar with the short-range movements of the King, you are ready for the next steps. They include King and Pawn (or Pawns) versus King (with and without Pawns).

Consider this position.

The basic concept involved here is the movement of the King. It is important to realize that, as the King moves toward a fixed goal, it has several equally short routes. One of these will be a straight line more often than not; but other equally short routes will not be straight lines. In chess, the old adage of mathematics comes a cropper: the shortest distance between two points may *not* be a straight line. The following examples will demonstrate.

It most certainly seems that, to reach the fixed goal, KB3 (that is, to capture the Pawn on KB3—and we're assuming the Pawn is *fixed:* i.e., cannot move), White must play: *1* K-B3, *2* K-Q3, *3* K-K3, *4* KxP—four moves.

Indeed, there is no shorter—with the factors shown. But that route can be an illusion, given other factors, say, an opposing Bishop controlling the diagonal which cuts through White's QB3. In such a case, even the odd way of *1* K-B4, *2* K-Q5, *3* K-K4, and *4* KxP is effective—and still only four moves.

So it is important to understand that the King has many routes. Consider the zigzag one: *1* K-B2, *2* K-Q3, *3* K-K4, and *4* KxP.

Here we refer you to the bit of advice previously given under "How to Study the End Game." Set up your own exercises for the King's approach, to be sure you understand the principle and not just the diagrammed examples. Actually, a King going from QB3 to KB3 has more than twenty different "shortest" routes! Work them out; then, for a given position, you will be intelligently able to answer the question which you must frequently ask yourself: "Which route?"

OVERTAKING A PAWN

It is seldom that the Pawn is "fixed." More often, in the end game, the Pawn is apt to be pushing resolutely on to queen —and win.

You can extend the principle of reaching a fixed goal, nonetheless, and so reapply the lesson just learned. The goal now will be the Pawn's queening square—or, if possible, some square along the route before it queens.

Having determined the square, you proceed again to study how it can be approached, and to this end the following problem becomes important. It is a wonderful example of how vital that question: Which route? can be.

The problem is a difficult one. Do not feel too bad if, as a beginner, you cannot solve it. But do try it first before reading the solution. As one important clue, consider that your King can have one of two totally different objectives.

White to Play and Draw

Stop! At this point study the position, try to determine what must be done for White to draw, and work out your solution(s) till you are sure. If you cannot succeed, then read on.

1 KxR! ....

Perhaps we could safely forego any comment here. And yet White's move represents a first crucial decision. Taking the Rook permits Black's Pawn to escape beyond the pale. Or, conversely, we may phrase it that the capture puts White's King hopelessly outside of the Pawn's square.

Suffice it to say, however, that the Rook must be taken: else, e.g., 1 K-R6? R-QB1, and Black has ample means for winning after 2 KxP, RxP; or even more hopeless is 1 K-R6? K-N3, and Black has made vital progress while White has resolved nothing at all.

1 .... P-R4

The dreaded Pawn advance. Still, the position is now one of King and Pawn versus King and Pawn. You can profit by reconsidering the current lesson—plus the clue mentioned.

Our clue was that White's King has two goals. One is to try to stop the Black Pawn. The other is to try to queen his own Pawn. The achievement of either goal will suffice to draw.

A brief consideration shows that neither goal can be attained by direct means. For example, the pursuit of the Pawn fails: 2 K-R7, P-R5; 3 K-R6, P-R6—and alas! the King can never re-enter the Pawn's square. And, as Black's King is within the White Pawn's square, 2 P-B7, K-N2 is equally futile.

As our clue suggests, however, we must try to use the White King to support its Pawn. On the face of it, this procedure also seems futile: 2 K-N7, P-R5; 3 K-B7, K-N3! and Black picks off the White Pawn with utmost ease, while his own Pawn will go on, unhampered, to queen.

White simply cannot draw, it seems!

The Solution(s)

Curiously enough, however, White can draw. His failure in the tries above results from his employing only the apparently shortest, the straight-line routes of approach. For the correct solutions (for White tries lead to more than one solution), you must fall back upon that vital question: *Which route?*

As White's King has two goals, the question now becomes which route will best serve both goals. By employing a route that advances the White King upon both its possible objectives in the shortest number of moves you can attain one goal or the other—and draw.

Here, then, is a striking demonstration of the value of the King's diverse routes to a given goal.

First Solution

Let us consider the correct route.

(Continue from last diagram)

2 K-N7! . . . .

By using a diagonal move, the White King advances with equal gain on each of its goals: to overtake Black's Pawn and to reach and support its own.

2 . . . . P-R5

Definitely Black's best try at the moment: his unstoppable Pawn hurries on to queen whereas White's queening is still out of consideration.

3 K-B6! . . . .

Again, a diagonal move, equally directed toward both goals.

3 . . . . P-R6

Black still presses on to queen. His alternative tries will be discussed presently.

4 K-K7! . . . .

Here, then, we see a use for the apparently senseless zigzag route described early in this lesson! The consequences now become fairly clear: White can reach and support his own Pawn, at need.

4	. . . .	P-R7
5	P-B7!	P-R8(Q)
6	P-B8(Q)ch	Drawn

For with Queens on both sides only a gross blunder can lead to a win now.

Second Solution

Admittedly, White has demonstrated a draw; but was it against Black's best play? What if Black tries to stop the White Pawn from queening?

(Continue from last diagram)

2	K-N7!	P-R5
3	K-B6!	K-N3

Black moves on the White Pawn before its King can arrive to support it. The Pawn is lost, surely?

    4   **K-K5!**   . . . .

Again, a diagonal move of the King is the shortest approach to its two goals!

    4 . . .   **KxP**

White's Pawn is gone, indeed; but now White's King is able to enter the square of Black's Pawn!

    5 **K-B4!**   . . . .

Within the queening square White's King soon overtakes and captures the Black Pawn: 5 . . . P-R6; 6 K-N3, P-R7; 7 KxP. In an actual game, the draw would be conceded now, if not sooner.

Other Solutions

These two main lines do not exhaust the possibilities. But enough has been stated to guide the way. You will do well here again to review "How to Study the End Game," as you should again and again in each end-game lesson.

For example, in the last line, note how White still draws after 4 ... P-R6; 5 K-Q6! by reverting to the goal of supporting his own Pawn on to queen: 5 ... P-R7; 6 P-B7! K-N2 [6 ... P-R8(Q); 7 P-B8(Q)ch is also a draw]; 7 K-Q7! P-R8(Q); 8 P-B8(Q)ch, Drawn.

And another interesting study is the solution with 2 K-N7, K-N3 in which Black goes after White's Pawn immediately.

Work out each possibility for yourself. The effort will repay you by instilling an instinct, as it were, for all such positions.

Principles in the Solution

Having worked out all the possibilities, your next step is to sum up the principles involved. Then try to remember the principles, rather than the moves—which may prove evanescent.

In this problem the outcome is a draw because White selects that King route which permits him to switch, at need, depending on Black's moves, from one to the other of two saving goals. Thus, in answering the question: *Which route?* the White King moves on the diagonal route: K-N7-B6 as it is quite as short an approach to Black's Pawn as is K-R7-R6 and has the added advantage of being a short approach to White's own Pawn.

The Diagonal Approach

In the question of the shortest routes to either of two goals, the King's diagonal move is most important. The beginner must realize, therefore, that the more "diagonal" the direction to a goal, the fewer shortest routes there are.

Imagining, of course, that the Pawn is "fixed," i.e., cannot

How many shortest routes are there?

move, there are only four "shortest" routes: (1) *1* K-N8, *2* K-B7, *3* K-Q6 and *4* KxP; (2) *1* K-N7, *2* K-B7, *3* K-Q6 and *4* KxP; (3) *1* K-N7, *2* K-B6, *3* K-Q6 and *4* KxP; (4) *1* K-N7, *2* K-B6, *3* K-Q5 and KxP.

In the following position there is only one shortest route, the direct diagonal: K-N7-B6-Q5-K4-B3-N2-R1 (KxR).

HOW TO STUDY THE POWER OF A KING

Put a White King and a Black Pawn on the board at random, and try to count the number of shortest routes.

When you reach a King and Pawn ending in one of your own games—*stop!* Try to visualize all the possible shortest routes. Decide whether there is any difference between these King routes and, if so, which is the most efficacious.

3

King Versus Pawns

THE MOST UNDERRATED MAN in the ending is the ubiquitous King. For a piece that reflects the climate of every move on the length and breadth of the sixty-four squares and for one with a powerful potential of its own, its appraisal is far below par. This is comprehensibly so.

In the opening and in the middle game a venturesome King is buffeted from pillar to post, and as often as not never reaches the post. In the ending, however, when most of the major pieces are gone and the risk of checkmate is therefore remote, the King can and ought to share the burdens of the ever-recurring problems. It is well, consequently, to establish the relationship of the King and other forces in terms of end-game powers.

In these terms, as an offensive and defensive unit, the King approximates the value of a Bishop or of a Knight, subject, of course, to the law that it may not be captured. While it does not exercise the long range of the Bishop or the devious hop of the Knight, the King attacks eight squares simultaneously in eight different directions. It is indeed, a weighty force, not to be discounted lightly or to be ignored in the culminating activities.

Kf or B up By c Active! king

KING VERSUS THREE PAWNS

It is a curious fact, though seldom put to the test, that a King can stand off and even capture three opposing, connected Pawns under given circumstances.

In the following diagram we must assume that Black's other forces, including his King, are somehow deadlocked. In such case, White's King, opposing three Pawns, must succeed in capturing all of them.

1. **K-N3** . . . .

This is the best move, although some others may lead to the same result.

1 . . . . **P-B4**

After *1* ... P-R4, much the same denouement results in mirror image as it were with 2 K-R4. But *1* ... P-N4 loses at once: e.g., 2 K-N4, and Black, being compelled to move, must advance either the Bishop or Rook Pawn to be taken. Thereafter, Black is again compelled to move, and all his Pawns are mopped up.

2	K-B4	P-R4
3	K-N5	. . . .

Now Black's Pawns are stymied. Black must pitch a Pawn and soon relinquish the others as well.

So much for the example. It is hardly, it must be admitted, of theoretical value. For positions in which the Pawns are so utterly on their own are few and far between. In this example it is to be noted that the Pawns fail only for want of one puny *tempo.*[1]

For example, after *1* K-N3, P-B4; 2 K-B4, P-R4; 3 K-N5, if Black's King could make one move, White's would then be compelled to retreat (obviously, 4 KxNP puts White's King out of the "square" of either of the remaining Black Pawns). Then a repetition of the procedure would lead ultimately to the promotion of the Black Pawns.

Because such positions are so very rare in which one side is so tied up that it cannot contribute even a *tempo* to the sustenance of its Pawns, it is safe to draw the general conclusion: three Pawns on different files will beat an opposing King.

KING VERSUS TWO PAWNS

Again, assuming the assistance of a *tempo* at need, two Pawns generally can hold the King at bay, although they cannot progress by force to the queening square.

[1] A *tempo* is the value of one move.

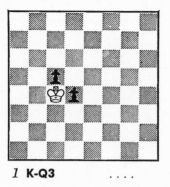

1 **K-Q3** . . . .

1 KxP is out of the question as the Queen Pawn runs on to queen.

1	. . . .	**Tempo**
2	**K-B4**	**Tempo**

The Pawns dare not advance so long as the King holds contact with the advanced Queen Pawn. It is a standoff.

In the previous diagram the Pawns were connected, i.e., on adjacent files. Here they are separated by a file. Yet they can still maintain each other with the assistance of a *tempo* at need.

1	**K-Q4**	**Tempo**
2	**K-B5**	**P-K4**

The advance of the further Pawn prevents the King from capturing the nearer: 3 KxP? P-K5, and the Pawn runs on to queen.

By jockeying the Pawns properly Black can always manage to prevent their capture. Indeed, *Black* makes progress if the King tries too hard: 3 K-B4, *tempo;* 4 K-Q3, P-B4; 5 K-K4, P-B5, etc. To hold his own, White must play 3 K-B4, *tempo;* 4 K-B5: another standoff. Black can't stand 4 ... P-K5; 5 K-Q4!

Exception to the Rule

When the Pawns are separated by a file, as we have just seen, they can sustain themselves against the King (with the assistance of a *tempo*). It goes without saying that distant Pawns, the two Rook Pawns, for example, can do even better. The King cannot chase down one without letting the other queen. So it appears at first sight that a separation of two files is even more favorable than of one. Oddly, that is an optical illusion.

1 K-K4   **Tempo**

On *1* ... P-QB4; *2* K-Q5, P-B4; *3* KxP, White's King is still in the "square" of the remaining Pawn and so can return and capture it.

       2 K-B5   **P-B4**

Now the Pawns hold as before, as *3* KxP, P-B5 leaves White's King outside the "square."

3 K-K4! ....

Now that the Queen Bishop Pawn has been induced to advance, the King returns, and for a purpose.

3 .... **Tempo**

If either Pawn moves, it can be captured safely enough.

4 **K-Q5** ....

Harking back a lesson, here we see most definitely that a straight line is not the King's most effective route. In a circuitous course, the King has vanquished the Pawns: *4* ... P-B4; *5* KxP or *4* ... P-B5; *5* KxP, and the King is within the square of the remaining Pawn. It will return and capture it.

A Practical Example

Theoretical exposition, no matter how interesting, is valueless unless some practical use can be found for the subject matter. Here is the case in point anent the foregoing discussion.

At first sight Black appears to enjoy whatever advantage is in the position. For it is clear that Black has checked the advance of White's Pawns for good. But it is not clear that White has checked or can check the advance of Black's Pawns.

White, strangely, wins.

1 **K-R5** ....

Threatening 2 KxP and staying within the square of Black's other Pawn.

1 ....   P-K4

Preventing the capture of the Rook Pawn. If now 2 ... KxP, White is outside of the square of Black's King Pawn. White's feint at the Rook Pawn seems to be in vain. Is it?

2 K-N4   ....

After having provoked the advance of the King Pawn, the King returns.

2 ....   K-N4

Black cannot advance either Pawn without losing both.

3 K-B5   ....

In any case, White wins both Pawns. The continuation might be 3 ... P-R4; 4 KxP, P-R5; 5 K-B4, and White picks off the remaining Pawn.

Exception to the Contrary

In most cases, with two passed Pawns on one side, counterbalanced by two on the other side, with each King within the square of the adverse Pawns, the game is drawn. This is so regardless of whether the Pawns are connected or separated by a file. The one marked exception is the position below. The point is: how far advanced can the Pawns be?

White loses as he cannot check the advance of the Black Pawns. As soon as it is his move, he must give ground. The King cannot hold separated Pawns which have already advanced so far as the sixth rank.

PAWNS VERSUS PAWNS

The most decisive factor in Pawn endings is the ability to establish a passed Pawn, that is, a Pawn unimpeded in its advance by an adverse Pawn. Where the Pawn position is unbalanced, that is where opposite colored Pawns are on different files, the positions abound with opportunities for creating passed Pawns. Where, however, the position is balanced, it is next to impossible to effect a passed Pawn.

Here is the classic exception to the rule.

With Black to move, the Pawns can restrain each other after _1_ ... P-N3. But it is White's move.

_1_ P-N6!   . . . .

This sacrifice effects a breach in the opposing Pawn array.

_1_ . . . .   **RPxP**

If *1* ... BPxP, Black fares no better. 2 P-R6, PxP; 3 P-B6, and presumably the Bishop Pawn goes on to queen.

2	**P-B6**	**PxBP**
3	**P-R6**	. . . .

The Pawn is passed.

WHY STUDY THE END GAME?

It is an axiom that one bad move nullifies forty good ones. As this applies only to the end game—after forty moves have been made—Q. E. D.

4

Know your endings! *Here it is White to play and win, not draw. Try to work out the win, first, then read text on "King and Two Pawns." Grow to know such endings as by instinct.*

King Versus King and Pawns

THE POWERS and proclivities of King and Pawns are strong and varied. We have already observed a few cases of their foibles. In the realm of chess, the oddities and curiosities relating to King and Pawn are many. They are, however, beyond the scope of this work, although by no means so for the scholar who aims for proficiency.

We expect to cover all the fundamental, elementary tasks and principles relating to the end game in the order of ease of assimilation. That is why we have begun with Kings and Pawns.

In this connection we begin with the proposition that King and two Pawns (or more) almost always will beat a lone King. The winning procedure is so simple that it requires but little explanation.

The object is to promote one of the Pawns to a Queen whereafter King and Queen can mate the lone King with consummate ease.

Hence, the Pawns must be advanced until one of them reaches the eighth rank, without being subject to capture. It does not matter, with two Pawns, if their King is not in the vicinity. The Pawns are self-sustaining (as was shown earlier), and there is always adequate time to maneuver the King to the required area. The first step is to bring the King to the support of the Pawns. Then the defense is helpless to deter their victorious march. Slight caution must be observed to avoid stalemate.

KING AND TWO PAWNS

The position pictured on page 29 illustrates the technique for promoting a Pawn, and the single hazard in it.

> 1 **K-Q5** ....

The King approaches to support its Pawns.

> 1 .... **K-R1**
>
> 2 **K-B5** ....

Trap. 2 K-B6 is stalemate.

> 2 .... **K-N2**

White's sole problem is how to approach without creating stalemate.

> 3 **P-R8ch!** **KxQ**
>
> 4 **K-B6** **K-N1**
>
> 5 **P-N7** **Resigns**

After 5 ... K-R2; 6 K-B7, there is no stopping the Pawn from queening.

KING AND ONE PAWN

In the studies of King and Pawn versus King, the principle of the opposition plays a major role. It is important to understand it thoroughly.

Vertical Opposition

Horizontal Opposition

Diagonal Oppositions

Distant Horizontal Opposition

The Principle of the Opposition

One situation that occurs very frequently in the end game is that of the Kings being directly opposed. They may be opposed in various ways, as shown in the preceding diagrams:

Three are all forms of simple opposition, with merely one square between the two Kings. If many squares separate the

Kings, they are said to be in distant opposition, as in the last diagram.

The critical point in any case of opposition is that that side which must move must give ground. Thus, in the diagram on vertical opposition above, if it is White's move, the King must either retreat to the first rank and so permit Black's King to penetrate to its sixth rank, or the White King must sidestep to the Rook or Bishop file and so allow Black's King to make headway on the Bishop or the Rook file respectively: e.g., *1* K-R2, K-B6 or *1* K-B2, K-R6. And therewith Black advances from the fifth to the sixth rank.

Or, in horizontal opposition, White to move, Black similarly can bull his way from the King file to the Queen file: *1* K-B5, K-Q6 or *1* K-B3, K-Q4.

So it is with all cases of opposition. The diagonal and the distant can be translated with due procedure into the simple vertical or the simple horizontal forms. In short, the side that must move must give ground; and, conversely, the side that has just taken the opposition is said "to have the opposition." Thus, taking the opposition is to secure an advantage and is often the surest and, in fact, the only way to make progress in the end game.

One Example

The importance of the opposition is well illustrated in the following position.

White to Move and Draw

Here we have conflicting aims. White is a Pawn behind; hence he strives for the draw. Black is a Pawn ahead; and he naturally tries to convert the Pawn to a Queen and victory.

With Black's King behind the Pawn and the White King in front, the correct play leads in nearly all cases to a draw.

Here is the procedure.

——1 K-K3 ——   . . . .

This move is not the only drawing move. 1 K-Q3 or 1 K-B3 will also draw, with the correct follow-up. But this is the best move, for it enables White to take the opposition no matter where Black's King advances.

1 . . . .   K-B4

To make progress, Black must play either 1 . . . K-B4 or 1 . . . K-Q4. If he temporizes with 1 . . . K-Q3 or 1 . . . K-B3, White returns (2 K-K4), and Black has not enhanced his chances.

2 K-B3   . . . .

White takes the opposition and prevents the Black King from making further headway. It is to be noted in passing that any other move loses for White. The exact winning method on another move will be discussed later on.

If Black plays 1 . . . K-Q4, White now plays 2 K-Q3, and the mirror image of the text occurs. The basic program remains the same.

2 . . . .   P-K5ch

Again, this is Black's only means of making progress. A retreating King move permits White to return (3 K-K4).

3 K-K3   . . . .

Here, too, this is not the only drawing move. Since it restricts Black's King, however, it is the best move.

3 . . . .   K-K4

There is no way to prevent Black from advancing. Fortunately, however, there is a way to prevent him from winning.

$$4 \ \textbf{K-K2} \qquad \ldots.$$

Again, the best move, but not the only one. The idea is the same as before. White is in position to take the opposition no matter which way Black's King advances.

$$4 \ \ldots. \qquad \textbf{K-Q5}$$

This time Black tries his luck on the Queen file. But it is of no avail against the correct defense.

$$5 \ \textbf{K-Q2} \qquad \ldots.$$

Taking the opposition. Black cannot progress without advancing his Pawn.

$$5 \ \ldots. \qquad \textbf{P-K6ch}$$
$$6 \ \textbf{K-K2} \qquad \ldots.$$

Here White's move is important as a misstep might be fatal. It is best to restrict the movement of Black's King.

$$6 \ \ldots. \qquad \textbf{K-K5}$$

Now again it is White's turn, and this time he must make the one and only correct move. Any other loses.

$$7 \ \textbf{K-K1!} \qquad \ldots.$$

So that White can take the opposition no matter where the Black King advances.

$$7 \ \ldots. \qquad \textbf{K-B6}$$
$$8 \ \textbf{K-B1!} \qquad \textbf{P-K7ch}$$
$$9 \ \textbf{K-K1} \qquad \textbf{K-K6}$$

Stalemate!

It is interesting to see what would happen if White made an incorrect seventh move. Instead of playing 7 K-K1, let us suppose he played 7 K-B1. Now White loses: 8 ... K-B6; 9 K-K1, P-K7 and, unfortunately, it is White's move. He must abandon the queening square by playing *10* K-Q2 and Black decides by *10* ... K-B7, followed by Pawn, queens.

Thus, it can be seen that the ending is no place to make even a slight slip of the finger. The difference between one square and the next may be the difference between a draw and a loss.

LEARN THOROUGHLY

It is not sufficient of itself to learn the drawing method we have just discussed. The type of position and the procedure ought to be so impressed in the mind of the learner that it is second nature. Only a fraction of a second at most should be required to determine the result. In this way all the profound calculation is circumvented, and a player is able to calculate a result with ease, even though he is far removed from the final denouement.

5

Know your endings! *Here, with an obvious advantage in space, White's King looks a sure bet to win the Black Pawn and promote its own. But see page 42!*

More on Kings and Pawns

Basic chess endings are many. Roughly, they number about six or seven hundred. Because a goodly number of these are more or less on the elementary side, they ought to be mastered by a reasonable degree of application. Yet such is not necessarily the case.

For every principle in chess and for every method there are numerous exceptions. Unfortunately, it is the exceptions rather than the general principles that rule. Sure knowledge of the exceptions is the line of demarcation between the chess player and the would-be chess player.

In the following general rule exceptions abound. Yet it is a good starting point for determining the result in King versus King and Pawn endings. *The King in front of its Pawn defeats a lone King.*

THE GENERAL RULE

The main idea is: the King in front of its Pawn promotes its advance.

White to Move and Win

White's goal here is to advance his Pawn to the eighth rank and promote it to a Queen. The method employed is straightforward and simple. The King clears the path and drives the opposing King from the queening square.

1 K-Q5 . . . .

White takes the opposition. Black must give ground.

1 . . . . K-K2

1 . . . K-B2 is no better. Then White progresses with 2 K-Q6, pursuing the mirror image of the following text.

2 K-B6 . . . .

Here is a major point within the main principle. When the King reaches the sixth rank, ahead of its Pawn, the Pawn will queen by force. It is important to remember this point to be able to foretell such winning positions from innumerable examples in earlier end-game and even middle-game setups.

2 ....   **K-Q1**

Whatever Black does, he is lost: e.g., 2 ... K-K3; 3 P-Q4, K-K2; 4 P-Q5, K-Q1; 5 K-Q6, and White wins presently as in the text.

3 **K-Q6**   ....

Here is the key square for the King, for the King can move later to either the King file or the Bishop file.

3 ....   **K-B1**

After 3 ... K-K1, White continues as in the text.

4 **P-Q4**   ....

White need make no calculations. With his King on the sixth rank, in the key square in front of his Pawn, all White need do is push. Push the Pawn as far as it will go.

4 ....   **K-Q1**
5 **P-Q5**   **K-B1**
6 **K-K7**   ....

White queens by marching 7 P-Q6, 8 P-Q7, and 9 P-Q8(Q).

ANOTHER APPLICATION

It is to be noted that, once White's King occupies the key square, Q6, it does not matter who is to move. White will win. In the previous line, Black was to move. Now assume White moves.

White to Move and Win

1 **K-B6**	. . . .

Or *1* K-K6 pursuing a mirror image sequel.

1	**K-B1**

On *1* . . . K-K2, White immediately assumes control of the queening route and queening square with *2* K-B7.

2 **P-Q6**	**K-Q1**
3 **P-Q7**	**K-K2**
4 **K-B7**	. . . .

The Pawn queens.

FIRST EXCEPTION

In the following position Black's King is in front of its Pawn; and, according to the general rule, Black ought to win.

With correct play here, however, White draws.

White to Move and Draw

    1 **K-K3**   ....

White takes the opposition, and Black can make no headway. Skipping mirror image lines, the text illustrates the general procedure.

    1 ....   **K-B4**

    2 **K-B3**   ....

By taking the opposition, White restrains Black from any progress. Now, if Black's King shuttles to and fro, White continues, holding the opposition: 2 ... K-K4; 3 K-K3, K-Q4; 4 K-Q3, etc.

    3 ....   **P-K4**

Now Black's King is no longer in front of the Pawn.

    4 **K-K3**   **Drawn**

THE RULE MODIFIED

From the foregoing we can adduce what amounts to a primary modification of the general rule: besides being in front of its Pawn, the King may need a free square between it and the Pawn. The modification applies when the adversary may otherwise secure the opposition.

White to Move, Black to Win

Between this position and the previous one there is but one slight difference: the position of the Black Pawn.

It is the slight difference, however, that makes all the difference in the result. Now Black wins!

1 K-K3   P-K3!

The Pawn advance places the onus of moving on White. With this extra *tempo*, Black secures the opposition, White must give ground, and Black goes on to win in the manner just discussed.

THEORY AND PRACTICE

Judging from what we have learned, the following position seems to be a win for White.

Black to Move and Draw

True, both sides have a Pawn; but, clearly, White's King will approach and pick off the Black Pawn. Then the King will remain in front of its Pawn, and White will win.

All is not what it seems, however. It is Black's move, and he has a resource also based on what we have just learned. By a deft stroke he can draw.

(As a secondary lesson, bear in mind that, although endgame combinations are comparatively rare, they do exist!)

1 .... **P-Q6!**

Since the Pawn must fall anyway, it offers itself immediately and so turns the table. White must now either capture the Pawn, by-pass it, or retreat his King. The other options are worse; so he captures.

2 **PxP**   **K-B3!**

3 **K-K4**   ....

Or 3 P-Q4, K-K3, and White's King is no longer in front of the Pawn. Then Black draws as already demonstrated.

3 .... **K-K3**

Now Black maintains the opposition and draws.

SECOND EXCEPTION

In almost all phases of the end game the proverbial exception crops up when there is a Rook Pawn on the board. It constitutes here another exception to our general rule.

When the King is in front of the Rook Pawn, the result is not a win if the opposing King can reach its R1.

1 K-N1   **Draw**

White's King shuttles back and forth between R1 and N1, and Black can do nothing to disturb these movements. Eventually, when the Black Pawn reaches the seventh rank, protected by the Black King, White will be stalemated (unless, of course, Black abandons his Pawn).

Try it!

AGAIN THE ROOK PAWN!

That pesky Rook Pawn figures yet another way in King versus King and Pawn endings. Here Black's King is in front of its Pawn, nor can White easily get his King to R1. In fact, it looks like clear sailing for Black.

White to Move and Draw

It would be, indeed, if it were Black to move. But it is White's move.

1 **K-B5!**	. . . .	

White not only heads for R1, the ultimate drawing goal, but also boxes in Black's King. (Look always for such dual-purpose moves in endings!)

1	**K-R5**	

1 . . . K-R3 is futile: White makes for R1. Nor does *1* . . . P-R3 change matters: White heads for R1 with *2* K-B4, and a draw results in similar fashion to the following text.

2 **K-B4**	**P-R4**

After *2* . . . K-R6, White has options: *3* K-N5, and he picks off the Pawn or *3* K-B3, continuing the policy of maintaining the opposition and boxing in Black's King. Either line draws.

3 **K-B3**	**K-R6**
4 **K-B2**	. . . .

White still heads for N1 and R1.

4	....	**K-R7**
5	**K-B1**	**P-R5**

If Black at any time abandons control of White's KN1, White secures his draw with K-N1. But, it seems, Black can progress comfortably enough with his Pawn.

6	**K-B2**	**P-R6**
7	**K-B1**	**K-R8**

Black cannot allow 8 K-N1; but he ˅an make way for his Pawn.

8	**K-B2**	**P-R7**
9	**K-B1**	**Stalemate!**

Even though a Pawn ahead, Black is stalemated!

ULTERIOR GOAL

When studying the endings, the learner cannot help but chafe over one goose egg after another harvested from mistakes in opening or middle game. It is difficult to see how improved end-game technique can remedy those errors.

To those who suffer from such sense of futility the only advice is: "Be patient." Perfect end-game technique will not only win end games. Eventually it cannot help but osmose to the other departments.

Know your endings! *Here it is White to play and win, not draw. Try to work out the win first, then read text on "Queening with Check." Do likewise, for that matter, with each diagrammed position, and the lesson will "take" more effectively.*

Hold That Pawn!

The cheapness of the Pawn is proverbial. Annals of all time are punctuated with such statements as "But lower Slobonia was sacrificed as a mere Pawn in the current game of politics." Masters of the chessboard, on the other hand, speak differently. One of the earliest great authorities, Philidor, declared that Pawn play is "the soul of chess." And Paul Keres told a member of the United States team only last summer: "The older I grow, the more I value Pawns."

Probably neither spoke solely in respect to the end game. But we must dwell upon play, both with and against the Pawn, in the end game. For here it is that the greatest power of the Pawn comes cogently into effect. In two senses you must hold that Pawn! You must preserve your Pawn to have winning chances, or block an opposing Pawn to avoid losing.

PAWN VERSUS PAWN

All other things being equal, Pawn versus Pawn results in a draw. The likelihood of complete balance, however, between the Kings and other factors is too remote. That is why it is essential to comprehend and appraise all routine and even apparently extraneous factors.

Who Queens First?

Who queens first is probably the most important factor. The race is generally decided on this proposition. When Pawns queen simultaneously, that is, one queens immediately after the other, the usual result is a draw. For Queen versus Queen with lone Kings on the board is a no-decision contest.

When one Pawn reaches the eighth rank and promotes to a Queen and the opposing Pawn reaches only the seventh rank, the Queen ought to win. Here is an example of the technique:

White to Move and Win

White's problem in this position is to prevent the Black Pawn from queening with immunity. To do so, White requires the assistance of his King, for a lone Queen cannot drive the enemy King from the defense of its Pawn.

White's goal, of course, is to capture the Black Pawn.

In the text position White dare not approach with his King, for Black will queen, and the game will end in a dràw. So the first step is to reach a position in which the White King can approach the Pawn safely. To do so, White must immobilize the Pawn.

There are various ways of accomplishing this objective. The quickest, however, is to bring the Queen in close contact with the enemy King.

$$1 \quad \text{Q-Q2} \qquad \ldots$$

Any move giving check and approaching the Pawn is good enough. The shortest route, however, begins with the text move, which exercises a pin on the Pawn.

$$1 \ldots \qquad \text{K-B8}$$

This reply is forced. On any other move, White stations his Queen in front of the Pawn by playing Q-K1, approaches the Pawn with the King, and then picks it off.

$$2 \quad \text{Q-B4ch} \qquad \text{K-N7}$$

Black, on the other hand, keeps open the threat of queening the Pawn. 2 ... K-K8 is a move which Black will make only under compulsion, for that move allows the White King to move.

$$3 \quad \text{Q-K3} \qquad \ldots$$

White attacks and threatens to pick off the Black Pawn. Note that White is utilizing various motifs to achieve his objective —the pin, the check, and the direct attack. Any one of these tactical weapons of itself would be insufficient for White's purpose.

3 .... K-B8

Forced, to defend the Pawn.

4 Q-B3ch K-K8

At last Black's King is shunted to blockade the Pawn.

5 K-B3 ....

At long last White's King is able to approach.

5 .... K-Q1

Forced.

6 K-Q3 ....

Because Black's Pawn is pinned, White is again able to move in with his King. Now, whatever Black does, the Pawn falls.

6 .... K-B8

If 6 ... K-K8, 7 QxP mate.

7 QxP ....

Because the White King in the text position was on QN4, in the vicinity of the Black Pawn, the winning procedure was comparatively short. Had the White King started, say on QR8 or KR8 or on any square a long way from the Black Pawn, the procedure would be longer. But the method would be the same: (1) Force the Black King in front of its Pawn by the pin, check or direct attack. (2) Approach the Pawn with the White King, whenever the Pawn cannot move. (3) Pick off the Pawn.

In this connection it is worthy of note that a Queen will win with consummate ease against a Pawn which has not reached the seventh rank, except, of course, if the Queen is subject to immediate capture.

Queening with Check

Another factor that often upsets the simple calculations of a Pawn ending is that one side queens with check. The check, which must be respected, acts as a brake in the routine procedure of the adversary. Here is a case in point.

White to Move and Win

There is more to this ending than meets the eye. Appearances favor a draw, but such is not the case. White has a way of jockeying the Black King into an unfavorable post which will cost him a move. And that move will be enough to decide for White.

1 K-Q4!   . . . .

Clearly, if White advances 1 P-R6, Black follows suit with 1 ... P-B6, and both Pawns queen with a resulting draw. White's King move does not appear to affect the issue. But it does.

1 . . . .   K-N5

If instead, 1 ... P-B6; 2 K-K3, White's King reaches B2, blockades the Pawn and then White queens his own Pawn.

2 P-R6   P-B6

Black has little choice. He cannot afford to lose time by moving his King.

3 K-K3   K-N6

Forced.

4	P-R7	P-B7
5	K-K2!	K-N7

Forced. Now we see the point of White's King moves. He has maneuvered the Black King onto an unfortunate square.

6 **P-R8(Q)ch**   . . . .

Check. Black's Pawn remains on the seventh and soon falls by the wayside.

Tail-end Combination

Another factor to be considered in the Pawn race for Queens is a tail-end combination. Often, after both sides have queened, a nasty check by one of the Queens results in the gain of the other. The decisive check may be administered on the diagonal, file, or rank, depending upon the position. Here the setting is in proper alignment for just such a conclusion.

Whoever Moves First Wins

If Black moves first, he wins as follows:

1	. . . .	P-R4
2	P-R4	P-R5
3	P-R5	P-R6
4	P-R6	P-R7
5	P-R7	P-R8(Q)
6	P-R8(Q)	K-B7dis.ch

Black's last move, discovering check, brings about the tactical motif known as the X-ray. White's King must move, after which Black picks off White's Queen.

With White to move, the win is considerably more difficult, requires an exceptional knowledge of technique. But the win is there.

1	P-R4	P-R4
2	P-R5	P-R5
3	P-R6	P-R6
4	P-R7	P-R7
5	P-R8(Q)	....

If Black now queens, White moves his King and discovers check, and Black's Queen goes by the wayside. Hence, Black tries to avert the discovery and hopes to promote his Pawn later.

5	....	K-B7

We now reach a tough position, somewhat ahead of schedule. In most respects it is similar to Queen versus Pawn on the seventh, already discussed. But there are some salient differences. Black's Pawn is a Rook Pawn, and this factor gives Black somewhat more leeway in the defense.

6	K-Q4	....

White's King approaches the Pawn and readies for Q-KR1, blockading the Pawn.

6	....	K-N8

Preventing the blockade.

7	Q-N8ch	....

Beginning a methodical approach to the Black King and Pawn.

7	....	K-R8

In the previous Queen versus Pawn on the seventh position, the King dared not move in front of its Pawn. Because Black has a Rook Pawn, however, White's King, as yet, dare not approach, for the result would be stalemate. Still, White has other means.

8	Q-Q5ch	K-N8
9	Q-N5ch	K-R8
10	Q-B4	K-N7
11	Q-N4ch	K-R8
12	Q-B3ch	K-N8
13	K-K3!	. . . .

The star move. Curiously, White could not prevent Black from queening.

13	. . . .	P-R8(Q)
14	Q-B2 mate	

Even more curious is it that Black could offer more resistance by underpromoting with 13 ... P-R8(N). Queen versus Knight, however, offers no serious problem for the Queen. Here the game is resolved by 14 K-K2, K-R7; 15 Q-N4, N-N6; 16 K-B3, and Black must relinquish his Knight and be mated.

7

Know your endings! *Here it is White to play and win. Try to work out the win first, then consult the text on the last example in this chapter.*

Two for One

THE REAL POWER of the puny Pawn is so great that the advantage of a single Pawn—all other things being equal—is usually sufficient favorably to determine the outcome of the most cluttered-up position. Barring blunders, an opening Pawn plus can be nursed through the middle game and turned into a potent, usually decisive factor in the ending.

It is in the last department particularly that expert treatment is required to avoid the snares, pitfalls, and swindles implicit in the position. It is at this time that the right procedure, even the right move, means so much, for one thoughtless move will nullify all the preceding laborious efforts.

The following examples will serve to indicate types of methods that can come up again and again. They are well worth knowing thoroughly.

THE LEAD PIPE CINCH

When two united Pawns, as in the following position, are pitted against a lone Pawn blockaded by the opposing King, the result is a foregone conclusion. The two Pawns will win with consummate ease.

White to Move and Win

The method is to advance the Pawns in a way in which they support each other, threaten in due time to queen, and draw the adverse King into their orbit. As the last action causes the King to relinquish its guard over the single Pawn, that Pawn is then picked off. In turn, the other King is freed to join in the queening operation, and the rest is what is described as "a matter of technique."

A DELUSORY PERIL

Even when the two united passed Pawns are apparently stopped dead in their tracks, as in this position, and the White

King is out of the "square" of Black's passed Pawn, all is not lost.

White to Move and Win

Even a couple of Pawns and a King can effect a mating net to win or at least to gain time by a well-directed jostle.

1 **K-N6**   ....

It is clear that an attempt to reach the Black Pawn is futile. K-B4 is met by ... P-N6-7-8(Q).

1 ....   **P-N6**

The Pawn cannot be stopped. White must act fast.

2 **P-B7!**   ....

This is not the only winning move. 2 P-Q7ch ought to win, too. But this is the prettiest.

2 ....   **P-N7**

What else? 2 ... K-Q2; 3 K-N7, and White queens *with check.*

3 **K-B6!**   **P-N8(Q)**
4 **P-Q7 mate**   ....

The foregoing position illustrates one of the rarer occasions with simplified Pawn endings in which strategy rather than tactics is the dominating force.

AN ESSENTIAL DIFFERENCE

Here it is to be observed that, if neither of the King Knight Pawns were on the board, the game would be a draw. But they are on the board, and this factor makes the difference.

White to Move and Win

A Pawn plus is usually a win in the ending, and the additional Pawns, even though well balanced, add to the winning chances. Hence the rule: when swapping down for a winning ending, exchange off pieces but not Pawns so far as possible.

Here it is two versus one, but the two White Pawns are separated. The general idea then is to draw the adverse King away from the support of its own Pawn. After that, the single Pawn is "easy pickin's," and the resultant position is a simple win.

1 K-B3	K-N3

Black has little choice.

2 K-Q4	....

White dashes for the other Pawn, while Black's King must keep the Queen Knight Pawn under close observation.

2	K-N4
3 K-K5	KxP
4 K-B5	K-B4
5 KxP	....

Black is miles out of bounds. So he resigns.

YET ANOTHER DIFFERENCE

Here is the very same position, with one notable difference. The opposing Pawns are on the Rook file, instead of the Knight file. Note we have mentioned that the Rook file is almost always an exceptional case. It changes the complexion of things completely here. The best White can do, with correct play, is to draw.

White to Move, Black to Draw

1	K-B3	K-N3
2	K-Q4	. . . .

Curiously, 2 K-B4, followed by 3 P-N5 or 3 K-Q4, gains no time.

2	. . . .	K-N4
3	K-K5	KxP
4	K-B5	K-B4

Black heads immediately in the general direction of his KR1. If he reaches KB1 in time, he can hold the game.

5	K-N5	K-Q3
6	KxP	K-K2
7	K-N6	K-B1
	Drawn	

There is nought to be done. On 8 K-R7, K-B2 draws as we have previously demonstrated; and, otherwise, Black reaches his KR1 and draws.

It is to be noted, however, that, if the position had been modified by placing Black's Rook Pawn on R3, and White's on R5, White would win. Black's King could not then reach any of the key squares in time.

By the same token, with Black's Pawn at R3 and White's at R4, White's only winning move would be *1* P-R5. If it were Black's move, his only drawing move would be *1* ... P-R4.

To determine the odds of any of these positions coming up exactly in a game would require the calculations of a Univac. Hence this study is meant to suggest a course of action for any similar position. It is not a static expedient just for the ones explained.

A BLACK DILEMMA

When two united passed Pawns advance upon an opposing Pawn and King, the result also is usually a win. The technique, however, must be flawless. Here is a classic example.

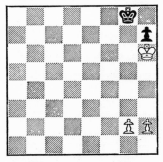

White to Move and Win

Clearly in this position there is no way of driving Black's King from the support of its Pawn. Hence, the winning plan must be to promote one of White's Pawns. The first step is to advance one of them to the fifth rank. It does not matter which Pawn.

| *1* **P-R4** | **K-R1** |

Here is Black's dilemma. At a given move it will matter vastly whether his King is on R1 or N1. Actually, his moment of dilemma is past, as White can now force the creation of the correct position. And, in syllogistic terms, it would have been a true dilemma; for if Black had foreseen and chosen to have his King at R1 at the start, likewise White could still bring about the desired position by force, or rather timing.

2	P-R5	K-N1

Now comes time for accurate timing. The right move will win; the wrong one will draw. The point is that White must eventually play P-N6 and exchange off Pawns. When he does so, he must be sure that Black's King is at R1, not N1. Here White has the choice of moving the Knight Pawn one or two squares. Which is correct?

3	P-N3!	. . . .

The only winning move. (Try the position, also, with Black's King at R1, and work out the results both with 3 P-N3 and 3 P-N4.)

3	. . . .	K-R1
4	P-N4	K-N1
5	P-N5	K-R1
6	P-N6	PxP

Nor does 6 ... K-N1 help. There follows: 7 P-N7, K-B2 8 KxP, etc.

7	PxP	. . . .

Now White has canceled the drawing outcome of a lone Rook Pawn. 7 KxP leads only to that draw.

7	. . . .	K-N1
8	P-N7	K-B2
9	K-R7	Resigns

Here we see the final result of the correct 3 P-N3! With 3 P-N4, the subsequent play would have offered Black the chance of 7 ... K-R1; 8 P-N7ch, K-N1; 9 K-N6, stalemate!

A FINAL FINESSE

Here is another example of two for one, with White's Pawns united. Unless White is able to utilize the theoretical information which he has gleaned from our studies, he can fiddle away his win.

White to Move and Win

The first move is the star move!

1	**P-Q6ch!!**	**PxPch**

Black can do no better. If he moves his King, White cleans up with 2 P-Q7(ch), walks his King to KB7, with appropriate timing, and garners Black's Pawn for an easy win.

	2 **K-Q5!**	**K-B1!!**

Trap.

	3 **K-B6!!**	....

Not 3 KxP which draws, after 3 ... K-Q1. Now the threat is 4 P-K7.

	3	**K-Q1**
	4 **KxP**	....

Now White has won the Pawn while taking the opposition, and the latter makes all the difference.

	4	**K-K1**
	5 **P-K7**	**Resigns**

8

Can White win? Work on this position for yourself first, then see page 71.

Pawn Plusses and Minuses

A MATTER of technique" is the phrase which, curiously enough, is applied to the hopelessly lost ending that requires no technique at all. Simple, direct, routine play, devoid of subtlety and finesse and brooking no opposition, is what this phrase depicts. To be sure, many Pawn endings culminate in such a manner.

Many Pawn endings, on the contrary, are full of tricks and traps and sagacious strategy. Sometimes their general contour is a carry-over from the middle game, when the strategic conception of the ending is already mapped out. Sometimes the strategic motif is introduced in the finale. In all cases, however, certain clear, identifiable characteristics predominate. And they direct the ensuing play.

THE PASSED PAWN

A Pawn unimpeded in its advance by an opposing Pawn is a significant characteristic. It is a dangerous Pawn, for it threatens to queen. Hence, it bears constant surveillance by the opposing King in King and Pawn endings. Thus it diverts the attention of the King from sundry other affairs. A passed Pawn, as a rule, is a strategic plus.

When such a Pawn is protected or capable of being protected by another Pawn, it is technically called a protected, passed Pawn. It carries a lot of weight.

Here is a position with such a Pawn. Units, it will be observed, are even. Black has a passed Pawn; White a protected, passed Pawn. The weight is by far in favor of the protected Pawn.

White to Move and Win

The first idea is direct. White heads in the direction and square of Black's passed Pawn. And Black is helpless to defend.

1 **K-B3**   **P-N5**

If Black temporizes with his King, say by *1* ... K-Q4, White keeps on approaching the passed Pawn, until he is in direct contact with it. At no time is the Black King able to defend the Pawn without stepping out of the "square" of White's passed Pawn.

2	**K-Q3**	**P-N6**
3	**K-K3**	**P-N7**
4	**K-B2**	. . . .

Now White picks off the Pawn and returns to the other side to win. While the win is comparatively easy, there are still some obstacles which must be hurdled. (See following diagram.)

White to Move and Win

1 **K-Q5**   **K-B2!**

There is a bit of jockeying here in order for Black to put up the strongest resistance. He strives for *2* K-B5, K-N2; *3* P-N6?, K-R3; *4* K-B6, stalemate. *2* ... K-N2 will not do on account of *3* K-B5, K-B2; *4* P-N6ch, K-N2; *5* K-N5, after which Black's Rook Pawn falls by the wayside.

White's goal is to queen his Knight Pawn or (first) pick off Black's Rook Pawn.

2 **K-K6!**   . . . .

White must drive Black from QN3. *2* K-B5, K-N2; *3* K-Q6 fails versus *3* ... K-N3, maintaining the opposition: *4* K-Q7,

K-N2; 5 K-Q8, K-N1. After the text move, White gains the opposition.

	2	**K-N2**
	3 **K-Q7**	....

White has the opposition. Observe the difference.

	3	**K-N3**

If 3 ... K-N1; 4 K-B6, K-R2; 5 K-B7, K-R1; 6 K-N6, Black's Pawn falls.

	4 **K-B8!**	....

Thus White circumvented the Black King and drives it from the critical field.

	4	**K-R2**

If 4 ... K-B4; 5 K-B7, White's Pawn marches on.

	5 **K-B7**	**K-R1**
	6 **K-N6**	....

The rest is "technique."

This simple ending illustrates any number of points. To begin with, it clearly exemplifies the power of the passed Pawn. Here both passed Pawns—White's and Black's—command attention. Only because the White King can reach the square of Black's isolated passed Pawn is the Pawn easy prey.

Because White's passed Pawn is protected and cannot be captured, it is both a latent and a potent threat. Yet, still there is Black's last hope, the stalemate trap to be surmounted.

THE OUTSIDE PASSED PAWN

A passed Pawn, as we have seen, demands constant surveillance by the enemy. An outside passed Pawn, or an outside Pawn, as it is sometimes called, is one which is even more dangerous than the usual passed Pawn. It is a Pawn outside of the squares of critical hostilities. Since it threatens to queen, it draws the opposing King away from any all-important sector and leaves that sector vulnerable to enemy penetration.

Here is a position with an outside passed Pawn in the making.

Black to Move and Win

A cursory glance will grant White the advantage, for he is about to win a Pawn. A second glance will give Black the advantage, for he can establish an outside Pawn. A third glance will only reveal the problems.

1 . . . . **K-Q4**

It seems that Black ought to make a dash to queen by establishing an outside Pawn with *1* . . . P-R4. For after *2* PxP, PxP, White's King cannot prevent Black from queening; whereas Black's King can prevent White from queening. This action, nonetheless, is superficial, illusory, and ill-advised, for after *1* . . . P-R4, Black does not win; he loses! White turns the tables with *2* P-B5, and it is he who establishes an outside Pawn: *2* . . . NPxP; *3* PxRP. Hence, Black must exercise caution.

2 **KxP** . . . .

On other moves Black wins with either *2* . . . P-R4 or *2* . . . K-K5, depending upon White's play.

2 . . . . **P-R4**

The purpose of Black's King move becomes clearer.

3 **P-B5** . . . .

On other moves, Black's Rook Pawn gets there first. And Black wins easily.

3 .... P-R5

3 ... PxNP will also do. The point is that Black's King can now take care of White's Bishop Pawn.

Thus we see how an ill-timed advance may convert a potential outside Pawn to an inside Pawn.

In the following position, White's Queen Rook Pawn is an outside passed Pawn. It cannot queen by force by advancing, for Black's King is within its square. But its threat to queen is sufficient to demand the attention of the Black King, which, in turn, leaves the Black Pawns as booty.

1 P-KR5 ....

This move effects a breach in Black's left wing.

1 .... PxP

Black has little choice. He must either capture, as in the text, advance his Pawn to N4, or counter with *1* ... P-B4. The counter is easily disposed of by 2 RPxP, K-K3; 3 PxP, after which Black's position is hopeless.

After *1* ... P-N4; 2 K-K4, Black cannot prevent the eventual penetration of K-B5. Then all of Black's Pawns fall by the wayside.

2 PxP ....

Now it is a question of timing. White's plan is to draw the Black King away from his own Pawns, and Black has no choice but to submit.

$$2 \ldots \qquad \textbf{K-B3}$$

The moves of 2 … K-K3 and 2 … P-B4 only delay the inevitable. Black's Pawns are doomed, and he must abandon them and hope that he can return in time to draw against a Rook Pawn.

3	K-K4	K-N3
4	K-B5	K-R4
5	KxP	KxP
6	K-N6	K-N4
7	KxP	K-B3
8	K-N7	….

Black cannot return in time.

THE BACKWARD PAWN

A Pawn that is behind its own Pawn on the file to the left or right and which cannot advance because it is immediately subject to capture and loss by an opposing Pawn is a backward Pawn. It is a chronic weakness in the Pawn array. Unless it can be dissolved, it usually creates a situation tantamount to being a Pawn behind, for then one opposing Pawn holds two in tow.

Here, with White on the move, he wins handily because Black's Queen Pawn is backward.

1	K-K4	K-K2
2	K-Q5	K-Q2
3	P-N5	....

Black is hopeless. His King must stop the Knight Pawn and abandon the others.

In the very same position, with Black on the move, the game is a draw, for Black can dissolve the backward Pawn with *1* ... P-Q4.

THE DOUBLED PAWN

Doubled Pawns, that is, two Pawns of the same color on the same file, are weak in the ending because the Pawns cannot defend each other. For practical purposes, the weakness need not be fatal when all the Pawns—both White and Black—happen to be in the same sector. When the Pawns, however, are separated, they are a serious handicap.

In the following example from actual play (Flohr—Capablanca), Black, on the move, draws by a quick dissolution of the Pawns.

1	....	K-K4
2	K-K2	K-K5
3	K-B2	P-R5!

This Pawn sacrifice is the key plan.

4 PxP   . . . .

4 K-K2, PxP grants White no headway.

4 . . . .   **P-B5**

Dissolving all the Pawns. White remains with a doubled Rook Pawn which is of no consequence. "The rest is a matter of technique."

With White on the move in the very same position, White wins: *1* K-K2, K-K4; *2* K-B3, K-Q4; *3* K-B4, K-K3; *4* P-R3, and Black must abandon his Pawns. Thus we observe that at best the doubled Pawn is rarely a virtue.

OTHER FACTORS

In Pawn endings, any number of factors, significant and extraneous, play an important role. Quantitative and qualitative Pawn structures, superior King positions, correct timing —all are part and parcel of the whole.

It is not within the scope of this work to document each and every one of them. One factor, however, which crops up sufficiently to demand attention is the Pawn mating net and the corollary threats which stem from this source.

An example to the point is given.

A Queen Ahead; Black Is Mated

The above position is a singular clue to the next one which is quite involved. A hasty appraisal discloses (1) White is a Pawn ahead. (2) White has two protected passed Pawns. (3) Black has a protected passed Pawn. (4) The White King is quite a distance away from its passed Pawns and will most likely not be able to assist in their advance.

White to Move and Win

The denouement rests on this last point.

1	K-Q4	K-N5
2	P-R4	K-R4

So far, so good. White has made a little progress.

3	K-K4	K-N5

Now it seems, however, that White is stymied. What is the next step?

4	K-K3!	K-R4
5	K-B3!	. . . .

In connection with White's last moves there are some observations. First, it is to be noted that the White King is still within the square of Black's passed Pawn: 5 ... P-B6; 6 K-K3, P-B7; 7 K-Q2, and the Pawn goes by the wayside.

Again there is a principle called triangulation.[1] White wishes to reach his KB3 to assist in the Pawn advance. Black, momentarily, prevents this action. White succeeds, however, by describing a triangle with his King—3 K-K4, 4 K-K3, 5 K-B3. This action places the onus of moving on Black, and White is able to make headway.

Triangulation is often an effective procedure for gaining or losing a move.

5	....	K-N3
6	P-N4	K-R3
7	P-R5	K-N4

Again White's Pawns are stymied. But the process of triangulation to the fore!

8	K-K3	K-R3
9	K-B4	....

White has again described a triangle with his King—K-B3, K-K3, K-B4—to place the onus of moving upon Black. Black must give way. Observe, too, that White's King is still in the square of the Black Passed Pawn.

9	....	K-N3
10	P-N5	K-R2
11	P-N6ch	....

White's Pawns have made rapid strides. As he approaches the goal of queening, the task becomes harder.

Here this question arises: Why did White advance his Knight Pawn to N6? Why did he not advance his Rook Pawn to R6? The answer is that White was acquainted with this type of position. The specific play does not originate with a principle. It originates with knowledge.

11	....	K-R3

[1] In order to understand triangulation, it is well to remember that a move can be gained or lost only if one King is in a to-and-fro groove while the other is able to move about freely. In the above position Black's moves were circumscribed.

Again White's Pawns are stymied. And again triangulation!

12 **K-K3!**   . . . .

This is not a retreat, appearances to the contrary. It is the beginning of triangulation.

White wishes to reach the position which just existed, only with Black to move.

12	. . . .	**K-N2**
13	**K-K4**	**K-R3**
14	**K-B4**	. . . .

And so White achieves his goal. It is Black's move.

14 . . . .   **K-N2**

Up to this point White has made much progress without risk. At no time has the King been out of the square of the Black passed Pawn. Now, however, if White is to win, he must be certain of what he is doing, for a misstep can be fatal.

15 **K-N5!!**   . . . .

The King is outside of the square of Black's Pawn.

15	. . . .	**P-B6**
16	**P-R6ch**	**K-N1**
17	**K-B6**	**P-B7**

Black's Pawn is enough to chill the ardor of an expert.

18 **P-R7ch**   **K-R1**

If 18 . . . K-B1, 19 P-R8(Q) mate.

19 **K-B7**   **P-B8(Q)**

White mates in three.

20	**P-N7ch**	**KxP**
21	**P-N8(Q)ch**	**K-R3**
22	**Q-N6 mate.**	

9

Can White win?—or draw? Study this problem first. Don't look now! *Not even at the page or titles. But it is covered in the next to last example on page 81.*

Knight Versus Pawns

THE TABLE of relative values of the chessmen gives a Knight as approximately equal to three Pawns. This is, of course, a rule of thumb, for the formula is variable. In the opening and middle game, a Knight, more often than not, exceeds three Pawns. Its versatility in leaping from one side of the board to the other in attack or defense is a plus trait. In the ending, however, three Pawns are usually superior. This is so as the position simmers down because latent factors take on an active role. The promoting powers of the Pawns, for example, assume great proportions. And, conversely, the Knight's mating ability diminishes to nearly nothing as it becomes a sole survivor.

Even the single Pawn looms menacingly as it enjoys a clear approach to the eighth rank unimpeded. In such positions, Knight versus a single Pawn, the question is can the Knight stop the Pawn by direct means by holding or blocking its advance? Or by indirect means which involve combinations? Usually, if the Pawn can be stopped by the Knight, one way or another, the result is a draw.

THE PAWN ON THE SEVENTH

When a Pawn is on the seventh rank, it is decidedly most dangerous. In the following type of position, however, the draw is easy. The Knight can hold the Pawn and stave off the intermittent sniping of the enemy King, even without the assistance of his own King (except for an occasional *tempo*).

Draw

1 K any	K-K5
2 K any	K-B6
3 N-K1ch	K-B7
4 N-B2	. . . .

Black can make no progress. The Knight will continue to swing, as needs be, between QB2, K1 and KN2.

When the lone Pawn is on the Knight file, the Knight movement is restricted to some extent. Here, for example, the Knight heads for N1. Should it get there, it will not be able to describe the previous motions. With proper play, however, the game will still end in a draw.

Draw

1 **N-Q2ch**	**K-B7**

If *1* ... K-B6; 2 N-N1ch, K-B7; 3 N-R3, the Knight cannot be driven from focusing on N1.

2 N-B4! ....

The trick clause. The Knight must abandon control of N1. Yet the result is the same. White threatens 3 NxP.

2 .... **P-N8(Q)**

Of course Black can promote to a Knight, but to no avail.

3 **N-R3ch**	**K any**
4 **NxQ**	**Draw**

The above position and this one are similar except for the location of the Black King. With the King controlling the queening square of a Knight's Pawn, the Pawn frequently wins. Here is one example.

White Loses

1 **N-Q2ch**   **K-B8!**

Black must be careful and actually permit the next check
rather than avoid it. For on *1* ... K-B7 White has *2* N-B4, as
we have previously seen.

2 **N-N3ch**   **K-Q8**
     Resigns

THAT ROOK PAWN AGAIN

The pesky Rook Pawn, as usual, introduces exceptions to the
general rule. Here, however, despite the limitations of the
Knight by the edge of the board, the Knight can hold the
Pawn, even though it is already on the sixth rank.

White Draws

1	N-N4	K-N6
2	N-K3!	K-B6

If 2 ... P-R7, 3 N-B1ch, followed by NxP, draws.

3	N-B1	K-B7
4	N-R2	K-N7
	Draw	

The Knight and the King can continue to play ring-around-a-rosy.

When a Rook Pawn is on the seventh, the Knight by itself cannot keep the Pawn in check against the incursion of the opposing King. Here White is helpless.

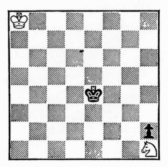

Black Wins

White can do nothing about ... K-B6, ... K-N7 and ... KxN.

Even against a Rook Pawn, however, there are tricks and traps, if the King can join the Knight in the defense.

Draw

Here, as before, the Knight is doomed. But another factor comes in.

1	K-B2	K-B6
2	K-Q1	K-N7
3	K-K2	KxN
4	K-B1	Stalemate

Thus we see that, if the defending King can land on B1 or B2 in the critical sector, the position can be held to a draw.

ON THE TIGHTROPE

In actual play the Knight and Pawn positions can be very profound. With all the knowledge gained in the preceding positions applied here, White can draw. But one misstep is fatal.

Draw

1 **N-B7!!** . . . .

1 N-N6 loses. *1* . . . P-R6; *2* N-B4, P-R7; *3* N-K2ch, K-Q7; *4* N-N3, K-K8, and White cannot avoid the loss of the Knight.

1 . . . . **P-R6**

Necessary. Otherwise the Knight parks in front of the Pawn with *2* N-N5 and *3* N-R3.

2 **N-N5** **P-R7**
3 **N-K4ch** . . . .

This is the key move. Observe in the note to White's first move that *1* N-N6 loses. The reason for the loss is that Black's King can reach K8 before White has time to set up for any kind of defense. Now the Black King is barred from that square for a sufficient length of time to grant White a defensive maneuver.

3 . . . . **K-B7**

If *3* . . . K-Q5, White sets up a barrier with *4* N-B2, for then Black cannot progress with *4* . . . K-K6 on account of *5* N-N5ch, followed by 6 NxP. Nor can Black progress with 4 ... K-K4 (to be followed by ... K-B5) on account of 5 N-N5ch, followed by 6 NxP. And, on other tries, the White King approaches the critical sector.

	4 N-N3	K-Q8
	5 K-Q6	K-K8

Reaching K8, after all. But one move too late.

	6 K-K5	K-B7
	7 K-B4	Draw

A KINGDOM FOR A HORSE

It is a well-known fact that a single Knight is insufficient mating force, if it is the only unit on the board (in addition to the Kings). It is equally well known that two Knights cannot mate by force, if they are the only survivors on the board. Paradoxically, if the adversary is left with some material, a Pawn or two, there are occasions even when a single Knight is a decisive advantage. Below is such a position.

White Wins

This is the rare exception to the rule. If Black were barren of material, the game would be a draw. But Black, unfortunately, has two Pawns and he is literally hoist by his own petard.

<table>
<tr><td>1</td><td>**N-B6**</td><td>**K-R8**</td></tr>
</table>

1 ... P-N4 leads to the same denouement.

<table>
<tr><td>2</td><td>**N-N4**</td><td>**P-N4**</td></tr>
<tr><td>3</td><td>**K-B1**</td><td>**P-R7**</td></tr>
<tr><td>4</td><td>**N-B2 mate**</td><td></td></tr>
</table>

A PAWN TO THE BAD

This is another variation of the same theme.

White Wins

Black loses because he has a Pawn.

<table>
<tr><td>1</td><td>**N-K4**</td><td>**K-R7**</td></tr>
</table>

Obviously, if *1* ... P-R7, *2* N-N3 mate.

<table>
<tr><td>2</td><td>**N-Q2**</td><td>**K-R8**</td></tr>
<tr><td>3</td><td>**N-B1**</td><td>**P-R7**</td></tr>
<tr><td>4</td><td>**N-N3 mate**</td><td></td></tr>
</table>

10

Can White win? *Here is a very nice exercise in end-game ingenuity. Alekhine solved this position in a matter of mere seconds; but it is not really that easy. Strengthen your own ability by working out the possibilities thoroughly; then, and only then, consult the text on pages 93–94.*

More on Knight and Pawns

O F THE MEN on the chessboard, the Knight is peculiarly unique. It leaps over all and sundry units, landing, as it were, on either black or white squares. Its singular leap taxes the imagination and renders the simplest position difficult of calculation.

One trait resulting from the Knight's leap is that the Knight cannot gain a *tempo*. Any of the other pieces, Bishop, Rook, or Queen, in relation to the King, can often steal a move, by correct, technical manipulation. Not so the Knight. If the Knight tours the length and breadth of the entire board a number of times, while the opposing King moves to-and fro, every time the Knight approaches the King, their relationship is exactly the same—and the same side is on the move.

This characteristic is not an asset for the Knight; it is, in fact, a liability. Yet it is something to remember in the final reckoning of the give and take of the essential computations.

EXCEPTIONS COMBINED

As we have seen, the Rook Pawn contributes a goodly share of the many exceptions to the general rules of chess. When the peculiar Knight is involved with a Rook Pawn, the exceptionals clash head on, and the men fail to cooperate.

White Draws

In this position Black is a Knight and a Pawn to the good. If there were any justice in chess, Black ought to win. But who said there was? Here there is no prodding White's King from its haven at R1. The approach of the Black King to R6 or to N6 terminates hostilities in a stalemate. And the Knight cannot move without abandoning the Pawn.

In regard to this and similar positions it is well to note the pertinent details. The Rook Pawn is on the seventh rank, guarded by the Knight. With the Pawn on the sixth and so guarded, Black wins. But even if the Knight defends the Pawn on the seventh from either B6 or B8, the result is still a draw.

QUITE ANOTHER INSTANCE

Now let the above position be inverted, so to speak, with Black's King in front of its Rook Pawn on the seventh rank, and a spare Knight in the offing. There ought, it seems, to be no question about the result. Yet there is a definite question.

How to Tell the Result?

Offhand, it seems Black wins. Actually, however, it depends on whose move it is. With Black to move, for instance, the result is a draw:

1	....	N-B5
2	K-B1	N-Q6ch
3	K-B2	N-K8ch
4	K-B1	N-B6
5	K-B2	N-Q5ch
	Drawn	

The moves can continue *ad infinitum* and *ad nauseam*. But as the Knight cannot gain a *tempo* over White's King, the result must be a draw.

With White to move in the same position, the story is different:

1	K-B1	N-B5
2	K-B2	N-K7
	Resigns	

White loses control of B1, must abandon that square, and free Black's King, whereafter Black queens his Pawn and wins.

The Easy Way

All well and good. Yet how is one to know the result of this type of position without going into extensive analysis?

Fortunately, there is an easy mechanical way. If the Knight can check the opposing King, the result is a draw. If the Knight cannot check, the lone King loses. When Knight and King are far separated, it is still easy to determine the result at a glance. If Knight and King are on the same colored squares and the Knight is to move, the result is a draw; if the King is to move, the result is a loss for the King. Conversely, if Knight and King are on opposite colored squares, the Knight wins if it is to move; and the result is a draw if the King is to move.

All this stems from the fact that the Knight cannot gain a *tempo*. A Knight on a white square moves to a black square and gives check to a white one. So, if the Knight is on a white square and the King is, too, with the Knight to move, no matter how far removed the Knight is from the King, the Knight will check the King as soon as it comes within checking distance. That is the guiding principle.

A One-move Pay-off

Often it is an exaggeration to say that the result of a game depends on one move. Here it is no exaggeration. It is the "honest" truth.

With the foregoing in mind it is clear that White must move both to confine Black's King and to a square on which it can

White Moves. Result?

be checked by the Knight eventually. Here, since the Knight is on a white square, White's King must move to a white square. *1* K-B2 draws; *1* K-B1 loses. Try it.

KNIGHT VERSUS THREE PAWNS

It is exceedingly difficult to generalize on an ending of Knight versus three Pawns. One thing, however, is certain: since the Pawns can hardly lose, the real question is: Can they win?

When the Pawns are separated and not subject to immediate capture, they are dangerous indeed. One or two Pawns tie down the opposing King, and the third Pawn, with the help of its own King, manages to trade itself for the Knight, leaving a winning result.

When the Pawns are together, as in the diagrammed position, they are dangerous, too. To determine the result, however, requires the most accurate calculation. Here, with White on the move, White wins; with Black to move, Black draws.

1	P-B5ch	K-N2
2	P-N5	N-Q4
3	P-R5	N-B6
4	K-B4	N-K7ch
5	K-K5	N-N6
6	P-B6ch	K-N1
7	P-R6	N-R4
8	P-N6	N-N6
9	P-R7ch	K-R1
10	P-B7	Resigns

With Black to move, he can draw with 1 ... N-Q4. The variations, emanating from this move, are long and laborious —as are, too, the variations from the winning procedure above.

It is beyond the ken of the average player to work out such positions to a conclusion, with so many moves to go and so many variations and sub-variations. The best advice is to figure the three Pawns as a win, particularly if two are already on the fifth rank. Then play the game on a move-to-move basis. Merely grasp as much of the position as you can and hope (and pray) to draw the game if you are the one who has the lone Knight.

A TRICK POSITION

When a King occupies a Rook square behind a barrier of Pawns, it is frequently impossible to drive it out. Hence, despite a preponderance of material, the result is a draw. Here is a type position.

White Wins

Superficially, it seems that White should win with ease. As a matter of fact, he does when he follows the correct procedure. But, then, what is the correct procedure?

At first glance the idea seems to be to sacrifice the Knight for one of the Pawns, then win with the extra Pawn. But try this on your pianola: 1 N-Q4, K-N1; 2 N-B5, K-R1; 3 NxRP, PxN; 4 K-B6 (not 4 K-B7, stalemate!), K-N1; 5 P-N7, K-R2 —and White must yield his extra Pawn, say, by 6 K-K7 or else 6 K-B7, stalemate, anyway.

There are other ways to mismanage to a draw; but White wins as follows:

<blockquote>

1 **N-B4**   . . . .
</blockquote>

Not the only move, but on the track of the only winning plan.

1	. . . .	**K-N1**
2	**N-Q5**	**K-R1**
3	**N-B6!**	**PxN**

Forced.

4	**K-B8**	**P-B4**
5	**P-N7ch**	**Resigns**

The point was to get to B8 (or B7) with the White King without stalemating.

THEORY VERSUS PRACTICE

This position from the recent Rosenwald Tournament exemplifies the winning procedure in an ending of three Pawns vs. a Knight.

Evans

Reshevsky

1	K-B4	N-Q7
2	K-K5	N-B6ch
3	KxP	N-R5
4	P-R8(Q)ch	KxQ
5	K-B7!	N-B4
6	P-K4	N-R3ch
7	K-B8	N-B4
8	P-K5!	N-N2
9	K-B7	N-B4
10	P-K6	N-R3ch
11	K-B8	N-N1
12	P-B4	N-B3
13	K-B7	Resigns

And here is the finale of another game in which White is a clear Knight ahead and ought to win. Yet his apparently valiant steed is nought but a pompous ass.

Nimzovich

Rubinstein

1 N-Q3? ....

The idea behind this move is excellent. Its execution, however, is poor. White anticipated *1* ... KxP; *2* N-B5, K-B5;
3 N-Q7 after which the Knight retains an iron grip on the
position. White's King then marches over to the critical sector
and picks off all of Black's Pawns. But now the game takes
another turn.

1	....	**P-B3!**
2	**PxP**	**KxP**
3	**N-B2**	**K-N4**

With a clear Knight ahead, it still seems White ought to win.
But soon an unusual position is reached.

4	**K-N4**	**P-K4**
5	**K-B4**	**P-K5**
	Drawn	

For there is nought to be done about *6* ... K-B5, followed
by *7* ... P-K6.

This is the way in which the game should have proceeded:
(See last diagram)

1 K-N4! ....

This is the key and star move. The point, as will be seen, is that White's King joins the fray a move sooner. This gain of a *tempo* makes all the difference in the outcome of the game.

1	**K-B5**

After 1 ... P-B4; 2 PxP e.p., KxP; 3 N-K4ch, followed by 5 P-N5, it is all over, for the Knight is immune, and White's King joins the action and decides.

2 **N-Q3ch**	**KxP**

Or 2 ... K-K5; 3 K-B4—the point of 1 K-N4!

3 **N-B5**	**K-B4**
4 **N-Q7**	**Resigns**

For Black is helpless against the incursion of the White King.

This delicate Knight versus Pawn end game could have arisen in a variation of a postal game between the strong Texas amateur, Homer Hyde, and his opponent, William Taber, former champion of several states.

Taber

Hyde

With White to move, there are yet a number of obstacles to be hurdled. The play would have gone as follows:

1 **K-Q5!**	....

The key move. On *1* N-B2, K-B6 is sufficient; and, on *1* K-Q3, K-B6, White makes no progress.

1 . . . .   **K-B4!**

On *1* . . . K-B6; *2* K-K5, K-N7; *3* N-N5, Black is soon shunted from the defense of his Rook Pawn.

2 **N-B3!!**   . . . .

The apparently meaningless gyrations of the Knight are the most purposeful part of the winning strategy.

2 . . . .   **K-B5**
3 **N-K2ch**   **K-B6**

Black's only chance: e.g., *3* . . . K-B4; *4* K-Q4, and White soon infiltrates.

4 **N-N1ch!!**   **K-N7**
5 **K-K4**   **KxN**
6 **K-B3!!!**   **Resigns**

Five star moves, and now it's all over, for Black's Rook Pawn goes, and the rest is easy. (Note, however, that *6* K-B4 permits a draw by *6* . . . K-B7.)

This miniature ending illustrates the Knight to advantage when used with precision technique.

White Wins

Before proceeding with the solution, let us analyze the problems involved. Black threatens ... K-N5, followed by ... P-R4-5-6 and the exchange of Pawns, leading to a draw. In the event that White by-passes ... P-R6 with P-N3, Black, of course, continues with ... P-R7 and P-R8(Q).

There are two ways to meet the threat. On the face of it, White's first try seems to be the answer.

1	K-K7	K-N5
2	K-Q6	P-R4
3	K-Q5	P-R5
4	N-B4	....

The further advance of Black's Pawn is checked. With a clear Knight ahead, the rest ought to be "a matter of technique." Yet even the combined brilliance of Alekhine, Capablanca, and Lasker will not win the game against best play for Black.

4	....	K-N4

Black takes the opposition and maintains it. And White can make no progress. For example, consider:

5	K-Q4	K-N5
6	K-Q3	K-N6
7	K-Q4	K-N5
	Drawn	

Any Knight move allows the eventual exchange of Pawns.

The Right Way

There is another way to check the advance of the Black Pawn.

(Resume from next to last diagram)

1 N-N3 ....

This move appears to be way out of context. Yet it is the only way. The idea is to continue with 2 N-R1. Then, when Black's King is at N5, Black cannot play ... P-R6; for White has N-B2ch, followed by PxP, with an easy win.

Hence, the Knight maneuver successfully staves off Black's prime threat.

But Black has plenty of fight left.

1 .... **K-B5**

Since that prime threat can be met, Black attempts an incursion from the rear.

2 N-R1 **K-Q6**
3 K-K7 ....

Even though far removed from the critical sector, White's King can join the fray in the nick of time.

3 .... **K-Q7**

The alternative 3 ... P-R4 fails: 4 K-Q6, P-R5; 5 K-B5, K-Q7; 6 K-N4, K-B8; 7 K-R3, K-N8; 8 N-N3! and White wins.

4 K-Q6 **K-B8**
5 P-N4! **K-N7**
6 K-B6!! ....

White can still go astray. Curiously, on 6 K-B5, Black draws by ... K-B6.

6 .... **K-B6**
7 K-B5 **Resigns**

Now Black can do nought to prevent K-N6 and the eventual fall of his Rook Pawn: 7 ... K-Q6; 8 K-N6, K-B6; 9 K-R5!

11

Know your endings! *Obviously, White cannot lose in this position. The real question is: Can he win? Study the problem first, for that is the best way to learn. But you will find the answer on page 105 in case of need.*

Bishop versus Pawns

THE TABLE OF relative values of the chessmen gives a Bishop as the equivalent of three Pawns. The formula is, of course, only a rule of thumb, to be modified by circumstances. In the opening and middle game, for example, the Bishop is usually more valuable. As an aggressive weapon, it can inflict greater damage than Pawns. And defensively, too, its rapid strides in reaching critical sectors quickly rule in its favor.

In the end game, as mating threats have vanished, the stature of the Pawns grows and that of the Bishop diminishes. Clearly, the lone Bishop, as opposed to Pawns, is at a disadvantage. The chance of administering checkmate is exceedingly remote, if not impossible. The only question is how much of a disadvantage.

Generally, a Bishop will hold one Pawn surely; two Pawns, likely; and three Pawns, possibly. As the Pawns grow in number, the task of the Bishop grows, too.

THE LONE BISHOP

The cases in chess history where a lone Bishop administers mate are extremely rare. But they do exist. Here is an illustration in point.

White Mates in Three [1]

1 **K-B3!** . . . .

The star move, releasing the stalemate. Without it, White cannot win.

1	**P-N8(Q)**
2 **N-B2ch**	**QxNch**
3 **KxQ mate**	

[1] This position is a composed problem. One of its curious features is that the movement of the Black Pawns can be reversed—and it is still mate in three! Only this time, the mate will be administered by a lone Knight. Try it.

THAT ROOK PAWN AGAIN

It is common knowledge that a lone Bishop, without other material on the board, cannot effect checkmate. It is not so well known, however, that a Bishop and a Pawn, opposed to a lone King, cannot win under certain circumstances.

Draw

As usual, the Rook Pawn plays its part in this grotesque result. Despite the preponderance of material, the White King cannot be budged from its haven at KR1. Any effort to prod him from that square by force will result only in a stalemate.

The features that make for the draw are to be noted: (1) The extra Pawn is a Rook Pawn; (2) The Bishop is of the opposite color of the queening square of the Rook Pawn; (3) The lone King occupies or is able to occupy the queening square. This combination of factors spells draw.

SIMILAR CASES

The following positions are all variations on the same theme. Despite material preponderance, the result is a draw.

Draw

There is no Rook Pawn in this position. But the Pawn juxta-position forms a barrier that is tantamount to the same thing. White's King merely moves to R1 and back, and there is no way to dispossess him from these quarters. The advance of the Black King to KB7 creates a stalemate. And the sacrifice of the Bishop for the Knight Pawn will lead to a drawn King and Pawn ending.

Draw

Here again Black remains with a Rook Pawn. This time, however, Black's Bishop does control the queening square. Normally, this position would be a win. White's Rook Pawn, however, prevents the Black King from approaching at N6.

Hence there is no way of prodding the White King from N1. Result: draw.

Draw

This position is unusual. The result is a draw because Black's Bishop is incarcerated. There is no way to promote its activity, and Black is helpless to make progress without creating a stalemate.

WHERE THE ROOK PAWN RULES

The following position has some of the earmarks of the previous ones. White has a Rook Pawn, and his Bishop does not control the queening square. But the Black King does not occupy R1, and with correct play cannot reach that square. This factor makes all the difference.

White Wins

1 **K-Q4!** . . . .

White's plan is profound. He is prepared to counter the advance of the Knight Pawn to N3 or N4 with 2 P-R6, keeping the Black King from reaching R1. This is the tactical basis of the move. Strategically, he intends to drive the Black King from the defense of the Knight Pawn, which he will pick off with his King. Then it will be clear sailing.

1 K-B5 will not do, for Black counters with ... P-N3ch, and no matter which way White captures, he will be in one of the drawing positions above.

1 K-B4 will not do. For ... P-N4ch creates the necessary access for the Black King to R1.

1	**K-B3**

In addition to the text move, Black has at his command the following moves: *1* ... P-N3, *1* ... P-N4, and sundry King moves.

After *1* ... P-N3 or *1* ... P-N4, White immediately plays 2 P-R6, keeping the Black King from R1, via N2. White then maneuvers his King to pick off Black's Knight Pawn and drive Black's King away from the critical sector: thus: *1* ... P-N4; 2 P-R6, P-N5; 3 K-B4, P-N6; 4 KxP, K-B3; 5 K-N4 (arriving in the nick of time to prevent Black's ... K-N4), K-B2; 6 K-B5, K-B1; 7 K-B6, followed by 8 K-N7 and the eventual queening of the Pawn.

Or *1* ... P-N3; 2 P-R6, K-B3; 3 K-B4, K-B2; 4 K-N5, followed by the capture of the Pawn by the King and leading to the same denouement.

Or *1* ... K-B1; 2 K-B5, K-Q2; 3 B-N8, K-B1; 4 B-B4, followed by K-N6, KxP, etc.

2 **B-N6**	**K-Q2**

If 2 ... K-N4; 3 K-Q5, followed by K-Q6-B7 and the capture of the Knight Pawn, with clear sailing for a Queen.

3 **K-B5**	**K-B1**
4 **B-R7**	....

Keeping the opposing King from R1.

4	....	K-B2
5	K-N5	P-N3
6	P-R6	K-B1
7	KxP	....

Black is driven from the critical sector.

EXCEPTION UPON EXCEPTION

The following position brings up some interesting points. With no Black Pawns as we have already observed, the result is a draw. If Black has only one Pawn, the result is a draw. But Black has two Pawns—too much wood for his own good. And that changes the picture.

White Wins

1 **B-K1!** ....

The key move here is based on tactical considerations. Black's King threatened to go to R4-5-6 and capture White's Rook Pawn or exchange it off.

1 .... **K-B2**

Now *1* ... K-R4 is met by *2* P-R3, followed by *3* PxP and an easy win, for the extra Bishop decides in any but problem positions.

Black is not concerned with losing one or both of his Pawns, for he would normally reach a stock drawing position.

| 2 | B-R4 | .... |

The basis of this move is tactical and strategical. If Black returns to N3, White wishes to be in position to check at Q8 and keep the King from R4.

Strategically, White has two things in mind. If he succeeds in either one of these, he wins. First, he attempts to stalemate the Black King. If he succeeds, Black must advance his Pawn to N6. White then captures, PxP, converting his Rook Pawn into a Knight Pawn, with a resulting easy win. Secondly, he attempts to drive the Black King out of the critical sector (its QR1) and to a point where he is unable to return in time. Success here grants White time to capture both Pawns before Black can reach the drawing position.

2	....	K-Q2
3	K-B5	K-B2
4	B-N5	K-B1

Black is putting up the strongest resistance.

| 5 | K-N6 | K-N1 |
| 6 | B-B4ch | K-B1 |

If 6 ... K-R1, a Bishop *tempo* compels 7 ... P-N6, after which 8 PxP wins handily.

7	B-N3	K-Q2
8	KxP	K-B1
9	K-N6	K-Q2
10	K-N7	K-K3

Black has been compelled to abandon the critical sector.

11	K-B6	K-K2
12	B-Q6ch	K-Q1
13	K-N7	....

Now White picks off the Pawn and wins easily.

The foregoing is only a rough outline of the possibilities of the position. To give every conceivable defense is beyond the scope of this work. Suffice it to say that with correct play, White wins.

WHAT, AGAIN?

By comparison, this position is an easy win, that is, easy if you know how.

White Wins

Curiously, without the Knight Pawn, Black draws. But he has it!

1	K-Q7	K-N1
2	K-K7	K-R1
3	B-B7	K-R2

If 3 ... P-N3 (or ... P-N4); 4 PxP (e.p.), K-N2; 5 K-K6, followed by K-B5-N4-R5 and the removal of Black's Pawn with an easy win.

4	K-B8	K-R1
5	B-N8	P-N4
6	PxP e.p.	P-R4
7	P-N7 mate	

BISHOP VERSUS TWO PAWNS

As a general rule, a Bishop can hold two Pawns. This position, at first sight, seems to be no exception. But it is.

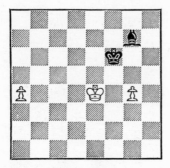

White Wins

| *1* **P-R5** | **B-B1** |

So that *2* P-R6 will be met by B-B4 with an easy draw.

| *2* **K-Q5** | . . . . |

To prevent the . . . B-B4 defense. The threat now is P-R6.

| *2* . . . . | **B-R3** |

In order to stop the Rook Pawn by . . . B-K6.

| *3* **P-N5ch!!!** | **BxP** |

If *3* . . . KxP, *4* P-R6 as the Black King interferes with the Black Bishop.

| *4* **K-K4** | **Resigns** |

For now the King interferes with the Bishop on another diagonal. There is no way to stop the Rook Pawn.

12

Know your endings! *Study this Reti position with care* before looking at text below. *How does Black win? Simply? Now take up the first example in the text below.*

Bishop(s) and Pawns

IF THE STUDY of chess could be reduced to axioms and principles, a twentieth-century automaton would make a mockery of the grand master. In less time than it takes to set up the chessmen the answers to the most perplexing problems would be produced with certainty and with accuracy.

Such, however, is not the case. Even what appears to be the simplest end game may, in fact, be a series of tortuous moves, embodying multifarious devious ideas interwoven in a plan which is yet part of another plan.

Take the positions with the Bishop and Pawns. On the surface it may seem that a few guiding principles should wrap them up. But there are principles and exceptions, and exceptions to the exceptions, so much so that it is better to withhold judgment. Particular positions are seldom wholly subject to generalizations. Specific situations have to be decided specifically.

A TYPICAL EXCEPTION

By all the laws of the Medes and the Persians and of chess, White is hopelessly lost in the photographed position above. His King cannot stop the Black Pawn from queening, while Black's Bishop can stop White's Pawn. Yet it is all an illusion.

1 K-K7!! . . . .

How this move affects the issue is decidedly unclear. The King even blocks the advance of its own Pawn.

So much for appearances. White now threatens 2 K-B6 which wins Black's Pawn, for 2 ... B-Q6 is countered by 3 P-K7. Black's reply is forced.

1 . . .	**P-N4**
2 K-Q6!!!	. . . .

This move raises a question: Is White a member of the Dodgers? For home plate is in the opposite direction.

But White is really on the right track, threatening 3 K-K5 to approach Black's Pawn. That Pawn must scamper.

2 . . .	**P-N5**
3 P-K7	**B-N4**
4 K-B5!!!	. . . .

The secret is out. By attacking the Bishop, White gains a precious *tempo*. If the Bishop is not saved, White can queen. If it is, then White's King is in the "square" of Black's Pawn and makes a timely return to catch it.

4	B-Q2
5 K-Q4	K-N3

Or 5 ... P-N6; 6 K-K3, P-N7; 7 K-B2.

6 K-K4	K-B4
7 K-B4	K-Q3
8 P-K8(Q)	BxQ
9 KxP	Drawn

A neat object lesson on how the shortest distance between two points may not always be a straight line in chess. If you really absorbed that lesson you could have solved this ending at the outset.

IRONIC INSTANCE

This Bishop and Pawn ending has a unique twist. Without the Bishop Pawn, Black draws. But there it is!

White to Move and Win

1 B-R3	....

It is essential to blockade the Bishop Pawn at once. Failure to do so results in a draw: e.g., 1 K-Q7, P-B7; 2 B-R3, P-B8(Q); 3 BxQ, drawn.

1	P-B7
2 B-B1	K-R1
3 BxP!	....

The trick play.

> 3 . . . .   **PxB**

On any other move the win is simple.

> 4 **K-B7**   **P-B8(Q)**
> 5 **P-N7ch**   **K-R2**
> 6 **P-N8(Q)mate**

It will be noted that the extra Bishop Pawn was a liability. It prevented a stalemate and, in turn, gave White the opportunity to build up a mating net.

UNDER TWO FLAGS

There is an expression that crops up in chess time and time again. It is "Bishops of opposite colors." It refers to one Bishop controlling white squares and the enemy Bishop controlling black ones.

"Bishops of opposites" is the boon and bane of the expert, depending upon which side of the fence he is sitting on.

Here, with two Pawns plus, because of "Bishops of opposites," Black is unable to make any progress.

Drawn

The Pawns are fixed on the wrong squares. White simply goes to and fro with his Bishop, and there is nought to be done.

Here is why "Bishops of opposites" are dreaded. With two Pawns plus, apparently on the right squares, White cannot win.

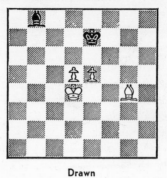

Drawn

Black shuttles back and forth with his Bishop. If the White King abandons the King Pawn, it will be captured. If White's Pawn advances to Q6ch, Black plays ... BxP, and White remains with a lone Bishop plus, for a draw.

AGAIN, THE EXCEPTION

This position is similar in some respects to the previous one, but there are some vital differences, sufficiently so to affect the result of the game.

White to Move and Win

For one thing, the Pawns are on the sixth, where they are extremely dangerous. For another, White's King can join the fray.

1	B-N5	B-R6
2	K-N6	B-N5
3	K-B7	Resigns

Black cannot prevent P-K7-8.

With Black to move in the diagrammed position, the outcome is the same. For example *1* ... K-K1; *2* B-N5ch, K-B1, and White wins by infiltrating with his King on the Queen side: *3* K-K4, *4* K-Q5, *5* K-B6, *6* K-Q7, and the advance of the King Pawn. While all this is going on, Black is able only to temporize.

LIKE COLORS

When Bishops are of the same colors, that is, they control the same colored squares (in the diagram, black), an extra Pawn often is sufficient to decide the game.

White to Move and Win

First glance here gives the impression of a draw. For Black's Bishop controls the queening square of the Pawn, and there doesn't seem to be a way of driving the Bishop from the diagonal. But there is!

1	B-R4	K-N3

Black's move is forced, for White was threatening B-B2-R7-N8, challenging the Black Bishop and driving it off the diagonal. Then Black has no defense: e.g. (Place White's Bishop at N8), *1* ... B-N8; *2* B-N3, B-R2; *3* B-B7! and White must queen perforce.

| 2 **B-B2ch** | **K-R3** |
| 3 **B-B5!** | . . . . |

The point of this move will become clear later on. Now, if Black could pass, White could make no headway. But Black is in *zugzwang:* he must move.

| *3* . . . . | **B-N6** |

Or other squares on the diagonal.

| *4* **B-K7** | . . . . |

Threatening 5 B-Q8, followed by *6* B-B7, etc.

| *4* . . . . | **K-N3** |

To prevent that threat.

| 5 **B-Q8ch** | **K-B3** |

Reaching almost the same position as the diagram, with one vital difference. Black's Bishop is now at N6, instead of R7.

| *6* **B-R4!** | . . . . |

Thus White is able to challenge the Bishop and swing over to the other side by the gain of a *tempo*.

| *6* . . . . | **B-Q3** |
| 7 **B-B2** | **Resigns** |

As previously mentioned, there is no defense to 8 B-R7-N8, etc.

A FUTILE BISHOP

As a rule, a Bishop can check two Pawns with the assistance of its King. Here the White King is on the borderline, just outside the critical sector. With precision play, Black can win.

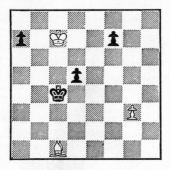

Black to Move and Win

1 .... **P-Q5!**

The star move. It is curious that the tempting *1 ... P-R4* will not do: e.g., *1 ... P-R4; 2 K-N6, P-R5; 3 K-R5, K-N6; 4 B-K3, P-R6; 5 K-N5, K-B6; 6 K-B5, K-Q6; 7 B-Q4, K-K5; 8 B-B6, P-R7; 9 P-N4*, and White draws.

The text move compels White to seek play on the other wing, for *2 K-N7* loses a *tempo:* e.g., *2 K-N7, P-R4; 3 K-N6, P-R5*, and Black jockeys one of his Pawns down to a Queen. The loss of the *tempo* exists in White's playing K-N7 and K-N6, instead of being able to play K-N6 directly. And the loss of the *tempo* is sufficient to turn the tables.

2	**K-Q6**	**P-R4**
3	**P-N4**	**P-R5**
4	**P-N5**	**P-Q6**

White is a move too late.

5 K-K7	P-R6!

6 BxP	. . . .

If *6 KxP, P-R7* wins. The winning procedure is an exercise in itself. Try it.

6	P-Q7
7 KxP	P-Q8(Q)
8 B-K7	K-Q4

This last bit of play on Black's part is worthy of observation. Strictly speaking, it is not within the scope of Bishop endings. Since it has come about, however, it is well to absorb the technique that is required.

9 P-N6	Q-B6ch
10 B-B6	Q-B4!
11 P-N7	. . . .

What else? If *11 K-N7, K-K3* wins in short order. Other moves will cost the Bishop.

11	Q-K3ch
Resigns	

For White must lose his Bishop or permit the Queen to go to KN1. When the Queen lands on N1, the Black King joins in the fray and White is helpless to resist for any length of time.

REPRISE

Here is another example of the triumph of two Pawns over a lone Bishop, when the King is cut off from cooperating in the defense.

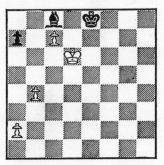

White to Move and Win

1 **K-B6!** . . . .

This is the all-important move. On other moves, Black plays *1* ... B-N2 and is able to set up a blockade.

1	**K-K2**
2 **P-N5**	**K-K3**
3 **P-R4**	**K-K4**

Black tries to reach the vital sector with his King.

4 **P-R5**	**K-Q5**
5 **P-N6**	**Resigns**

Black is out of bounds. There is no defense.

A PRACTICAL EXAMPLE

All the basic theory in the world hardly touches the experience of over-the-board play. The following position occurred between two masters, and more than twenty hours of analysis were spent over it, before the final winning procedure was discovered. Almost inconceivable in such a simple setting.

A study of the position discloses that White cannot force his passed Pawn to a Queen. Hence, he must capture Black's Pawn. In doing so, however, he will necessarily relinquish his own passed Pawn. Then the question will remain, will White's last remaining Pawn be sufficient to win?

The first question for White to decide in capturing Black's Pawn is where the White King belongs, for it might be stationed at K5, at B6, at N5, or even at N6. If one decided merely by intuition, rather than by cold analysis, the answer would be the King belongs on N6, before effecting the capture of the Black Pawn. For N6 is closer to the queening square of the Bishop Pawn. Yet that would be the incorrect answer.

1 K-K5 . . . .

Attacking the Pawn, and with a winning threat. White threatens 2 B-N2 and, while Black temporizes, 3 K-B6, 4 K-N5 and 5 B-K4. Then Black is in an embarrassing position, for if he captures the Bishop, he is in a losing Pawn ending. And if he fails to capture the Bishop, White plays BxP, and gains a vital *tempo* by attacking Black's Bishop.

1 . . . .   **B-R6**

To prevent White's threat.

2 **B-K6** . . . .

White plays immediately to win the Bishop Pawn for his Knight Pawn.

How does he know that he shouldn't play his King to some other square before winning the Pawn? He knows only because he has analyzed the position. His King belongs on K5 for a reason that will become apparent many moves later.

2 . . . .   **K-N2**

3 **BxP**   **B-B8**

Of course not 3 . . . B-N7 because of 4 B-K4ch forcing the exchange of Bishops.

4 **B-Q6!!** . . . .

All part and parcel of the winning plan.

4 . . . .   **B-Q6**

This seems to be the best try for Black, yet the game is soon over. The line offering the most resistance is 4 . . . KxP. Then, however, White wins by advancing his Pawn to B5 and B6, placing his Bishop at B7 so as to prevent the adverse King from getting to KB1 and following through by getting his King to KN7, reaching a position similar to the previous one. All this is a long and arduous procedure. But White wins.

5 **K-Q4!** . . . .

The secret is out. Why K-K5, when capturing the Pawn? Because now the White King can attack the Black Bishop. From any of the other squares—B6, N5, N6—he couldn't attack the Black Bishop. And why attack the Bishop?

5 . . . .   **B moves**

6 **K-B5**   **Resigns**

White, by the attack on the Bishop, has gained the necessary *tempo* to defend his second Pawn. With two Pawns up and with Bishops of the same color, the win is easy.

Q. E. D.

13

Know your endings! *Exceptions and counter-principles seem to rule in chess, in the endings as well as elsewhere. Here the long-range Bishop traverses the path of White's Pawn, a point in its favor. Can, then, the short-stepping Knight reinforce the Pawn decisively? See last example in text.*

Bishop versus Knight

THEORY has fluctuated on the relative merits of Bishop and Knight. About a century ago the Knight in all its pristine glory was in favor. As the science of chess progressed, the trial-and-error method evoked a reappraisal, and the Bishop ruled supreme. Contemporary experts lean toward the Bishop, though not so radically.

The Bishop is a long-range piece. It attacks and defends

from a distance, crossing the length and breadth of the board in a single move. The Bishop is restricted, however, to one color. On the white squares it is always on the white squares; or, if it starts on the black, it must remain on black.

The inimitable Knight's move is akin to a hop and skip. It is capable, however, of covering both black and white squares. A vital difference.

To level off the comparison, it is important to note that the Bishop is able, more often than not, to gain a *tempo* in relation to the Knight or to a semi-restricted King. The peculiar leap of the Knight does not embrace this quality.

THE THESIS

That the Bishop is infinitesimally stronger than the Knight is, after all, a matter of opinion, for there is no mathematical formula which leads to this conclusion. Only the test of grueling over-the-board play is a confirmation.

PART 1—PRO BISHOP

A Critical Example

The following position is an excellent example to make the point. It is well balanced in that each side has an equal number of Pawns in the east and west sectors. It is from the game, Stoltz-Kashdan, The Hague, 1928.

1 . . . .   K-B1

Black moves first. As a matter of good strategy, he begins to centralize his King, from which point of vantage the King will have easy access to either side of the board.

$$2 \quad \textbf{K-B1} \quad \quad \dots$$

White follows suit.

2	....	**K-K2**
3	**K-K2**	**K-Q3**
4	**K-Q3**	**K-Q4**

Black arrives first, and White is on the defensive.

It may be argued here that the important distinction of the position is not the Bishop versus the Knight but, instead, the initiative of the first King move. There is, of course, much truth in the argument. If White had moved first, to be sure, White would not lose. Neither would he win. Yet Black is able to convert the slim advantage of the first move to a win!

From here on Black must make progress. The general plan is to weaken White's King-side Pawn configuration, invade and rout it, and tie on to White's Queen Knight Pawn and cause it to fall.

Because the Bishop is able to gain a *tempo* over the Knight, when needed, White cannot maintain the present position. He will be compelled to give ground, permitting Black's King to enter at its K5 or on the Queen side at a critical moment.

$$5 \quad \textbf{P-R4} \quad \quad \dots$$

White may assume any number of different Pawn formations, each of which is implicitly weak. The text move aims to cut down on Black's Pawn *tempi* and, at the same time, put the Pawn on black, where it is less vulnerable to the Bishop.

$$5 \quad \dots \quad \quad \textbf{B-B1}$$

This inane-looking move is actually purposeful. To begin with, it throws the onus of the move on White, who becomes

more and more hard pressed for good moves. In other words,
Black is able to stall, and White is not. In addition, Black
threatens ... B-R3 and an incursion from the rear.

6 N-B3   ....

There is no good way of keeping the Bishop out. If 6 P-QN4,
B-R3ch; 7 P-N5, B-N2, White's Queen Knight Pawn is doomed.

6	**B-R3ch**
7 **K-B3**	....

Or 7 K-K3, K-B4; 8 N-N5, K-N5; 9 NxBP, KxP and Black's
Queen Rook Pawn will march on unimpeded.

7	**P-R3**

To prevent 8 N-N5.

8 **N-Q4**	**P-N3**

To prevent 9 N-B5.

9 **N-B2**	**K-K5**

At long last, a step forward.

10 **N-K3**	**P-B4**
11 **K-Q2**	**P-B5**
12 **N-N4**	**P-R4**

White's defense gets more difficult.

13 N-B6ch   ....

13 N-R2 seems to offer more resistance. Even then 13 ...
B-N4; 14 K-B3, B-K7 leaves White at a loss.

13	**K-B4**
14 **N-Q7**	**B-B1!**
15 **N-B8**	....

White is pinning on to any target...

15 ....   **P-N4**

...but it is of no avail. Now there is danger of the Knight going lost.

16 **P-N3**   ....

Necessary. *16* PxP, KxP, and the Knight is lost.

16 ....   **PxRP**

17 **PxRP**   **K-N5**

18 **N-N6**   **B-B4**

Now a Pawn goes by the wayside. It is practically over.

19 **N-K7**   **B-K3**

20 **P-N4**   **KxP**

21 **K-Q3**   **K-N5**

Black must exercise a bit of care and precision.

22 **K-K4**   **P-R5**

23 **N-B6**   **B-B4ch**

24 **K-Q5**   **P-B6**

To avoid *25* N-K5ch, followed by *26* N-B3.

25 **P-N5**   **P-R6**

26 **NxP**   **P-R7**

27 **P-N6**   **P-R8(Q)**

White shortly resigned.

Thus the peregrinations of the Bishop have won out. But only by the slimmest of margins.

Range as a Factor

The long-distance range of the Bishop often can be utilized not only to further the advance of the Pawn, but also to tie up the Knight completely. Here is a case in point.

If 2 ... B-R5; 3 N-N4, B-Q1; 4 N-B6 wins.

3 **N-N4**	**K-R1** [1]
4 **N-B6**	**Resigns**

The Bishop must abandon the all-important diagonal.

Observe the feature of this end game which makes the win possible. It is Black's King, incarcerated in the corner. If, at the critical moment, the King were able to move, White could not force the win. But because of this, Black is literally in *zugzwang*.

CONCLUSION

In the greater number of instances here the Knight has prevailed. Lest we mislead the reader, we hasten to state that, in the general rule, the Bishop holds the edge.

As the general rule is more easily stated, it is readily absorbed and then taken for granted. So its instances become less noteworthy. Nonetheless, the general rule—here the Bishop—does prevail.

Still, in chess the exceptional is important. And instances in which the Knight prevails, like the irregular verbs in French, crop up in so many different guises that one must never unthinkingly underestimate the power of the Knight.

[1] 3 ...   B-N4 may hold the game!

14

Know your endings! *White on the move; who wins? Try to solve position first, then see last example.*

Rook versus Pawns

IT IS A well-known fact that a Rook is much stronger than a Pawn. Five times as strong, to be exact, in the normal position. When an ending is reached, however, and mating threats are subdued, the Pawn comes into its own. With each advance toward the eighth rank, the Pawn looms as a greater menace, for the eighth rank usually means the conversion from Pawn to Queen; and there is no greater power on the chessboard than the Queen. It is this potential, ever-changing value which ennobles the Pawn and so creates conflict between units of such unlike stature.

When two or more Pawns oppose a Rook in an ending, the play is often tenuous. The difference between a win, a draw, and a loss is the location of the adverse Kings. When the superior King is within the orbit of the opposing Pawns, the King and Rook, operating in concert, mop up the Pawns. When the superior King, however, is on the borderline or out of reach of the Pawn(s), and when, above all, the inferior King lends support to the Pawn(s), the play is treacherous and exacting.

PART 1—ROOK VERSUS PAWN

A Model Ending—and a Refinement

The usual way of ending the career of an ambitious Pawn is to bring the superior King within its "square" and pick it off. That method works here by *1* K-N5, *2* K-B4, *3* K-Q3 heading for KN2. But it happens to be the arduous way. There is a simpler.

1 **R-N1ch!** . . . .

The essence here is to gain time by forcing the adverse King back. As it must then return to further the advance of the Pawn, White's net gain is one of several moves.

1 . . . . **K-B4**

To be able to protect the Pawn in the event of 2 R-KR1.

2 **R-KR1**   **K-N3**

The Pawn is protected but Black's King is set back two squares.

3 **K-N5**   **P-R4**
4 **K-B4**   **K-N4**
5 **K-Q3**   **K-N5**

White's gain of time enables him to reach the goal with a move in hand.

6 **K-K2**   **P-R5**
7 **K-B2**   **P-R6**
8 **R-R1**   **Resigns**

For Black's King is soon driven from the defense of the Pawn.

The Model Ending

Still, as an exercise, it is important to know what happens in the model ending with a direct approach.

(Start from previous diagram)

1 **K-N5**   **P-R4**
2 **K-B4**   **P-R5**
3 **K-Q3**   **K-N6**

Or 3 ... P-R6; 4 K-K2, K-N6 reverts to the same position as in the next note.

4 **K-K2**   **K-N7**

On 4 ... P-R6, White's job is comparatively simple: 5 K-B1, P-R7 (or 5 ... K-R7; 6 R-R3 and mate next); 6 R-R3ch, and Black's Pawn must fall.

5 **R-R8**   **P-R6**
6 **R-N8ch**   . . . .

Note the classic use of the Rook: it works from behind the King and Pawn.

6	**K-R8**
7 **K-B2**	**P-R7**
8 **K-N3!**	....

White releases the stalemate.

8	**K-N8**
9 **K-R3dis.ch**	**K-R8**
10 **R-QR8**	**Resigns**

For, after *11* R-R1ch, White picks off the Pawn.

Another Pawn Pursuit

Here is another version of a Pawn chase by an enemy King and Rook.

But because the Pawn is on the third rank, the winning technique is much simpler than first appears.

1 **R-R5!** ....

This is an attempt to fix the opposing King on its third rank. On this rank it cannot support the Pawn on the sixth rank and beyond.

1	**P-N4**
2 **K-Q7**	....

The White King approaches, and it is a matter of time before the Pawn is picked off.

2 ....   P-N5

Black is lost no matter how he proceeds: e.g., 2 ... K-N3 (to use the Pawn as a shield for crossing over at Black's KR4); 3 K-K6, K-R4; 4 K-B5 after which the Pawn is a "gone gosling."

3 K-Q6   ....

White need not be perturbed about any further advance of the Pawn. For after 3 ... P-N6; 4 R-R3, P-N7; 5 R-KN3, the Pawn falls.

3 ....   K-N3

Black only marks time, since he cannot advance the Pawn.

4 R-K5   ....

Other moves will do, too, but this one is thematic. White's plan is to pick off the Black Pawn with the King. 4 K-K5 interferes with the Rook and permits Black's King to go to N4. After the text move, Black's King is still fixed on the third rank.

4 ....   K-B3
5 K-Q5   Resigns

For, as already noted, 5 ... P-N6 is met by 6 R-K3, P-N7; 7 R-KN3. On other temporizing moves, White gets his King, via Q4, to the opposing Pawn.

A Finesse

There are many ways of skinning a Pawn in Rook versus Pawn endings. Here, for example, the White King is out of bounds, or apparently so, and the Black King is in position to support the advance of the Pawn. By delicate tactics, however, the Rook can triumph.

1 R-Q2 . . . .

It is clear that the Rook must move. Why to Q2 is the perplexing question. The point will become clear as the play progresses.

1 . . . . **P-Q5**

Not *1* . . . K-K5; *2* K-Q6, P-Q5; *3* K-B5, P-Q6; *4* K-B4, as the Pawn goes lost.

2 R-Q1! . . . .

The point. White actually took two moves—on purpose—to reach Q1, when he might have done so in one move. In this way he obtains the position he is seeking while he still maintains the opposition with his King. The King opposition is essential to make successful progress.

2 . . . . **K-Q4**

Black tries to circumscribe the White King from the critical sector.

3 K-Q7! . . . .

By maintaining the opposition, White forces Black to give ground. Observe that, if Black could maintain the opposition,

White's King could not advance soon enough to count in the immediate proceedings.

Observe, too, that 3 K-B6 will not do. 3 ... K-K5; 4 K-K6, P-Q6, and Black has the opposition.

	3	**K-K5**

Or 3 ... K-B5; 4 K-K6. In either case, the Pawn soon falls.

4	**K-B6**	**P-Q6**
5	**K-B5**	**K-K6**
6	**K-B4**	**P-Q7**

One move too late.

7	**K-B3**	**Resigns**

PART 2—ROOK VERSUS PAWNS

A Critical Point

This position points up the danger of two connected passed Pawns pitted against a Rook. When the Pawns are on the sixth rank, the Pawns will beat a Rook, generally, when both Kings are out of the critical sector.

White Wins

1	**P-B6**	**K-B2**
2	**P-N7**	**R-KN4**
3	**P-B7**	**Resigns**

For there is no way of preventing queening; and a Queen wins against a Rook with a reasonable degree of ease.

An Exception to the Point

To be sure there are exceptions to almost every principle in chess. This position contradicts the previous one. Black has two Pawns on the sixth, which ought to beat the Rook. Yet the Rook wins.

The Pawns and the Rook are, indeed, the overshadowing factors of this position. But the positions of the Kings, too, play a leading role. Here, curiously, the Black King is at a disadvantage.

White Wins

1 **R-Q2ch!!** . . . .

To force the King to the first rank.

1 . . . . **K-N8**

Obviously, if King to the sixth rank, then 2 R-Q3ch, followed by RxP, etc. And if *1* ... K-R8; 2 K-N3, Black is mated next move.

2 **K-B3!!!** . . . .

This move places the White King in the proper position for subsequent action, as will be seen.

2 . . . . **K-B8**

Of course, if 2 ... K-R8; 3 K-N3, mate follows, as already noted. If, however, 2 ... P-N7; 3 R-Q1ch, K-R7; 4 R-KN1, P-R7 (4 ... K-R6; 5 R-R1 mate); 5 RxPch, followed by RxP, etc. Also, if 2 ... P-R7; 3 R-Q1ch, K-R7; 4 R-KR1, P-N7; 5 RxP, the Knight Pawn is pinned and falls.

3 R-QR2   K-Q8

If 3 ... K-N8; 4 R-K2 forces the variations given in the note to Black's 2 ... K-B8.

4 K-Q3   K-B8

Black is wriggling and squirming out of the mating threat. If 4 ... K-K8 instead, 5 K-K3, threatens mate, and the White King then approaches the Black Pawns and is able to pick them off.

5 K-K3   . . . .

Approaching the Pawns with a view to capturing them.

5 . . . .   P-R7

Or 5 ... P-N7; 6 K-B2, and White's King controls the Pawns.

6 R-R1ch   K-N7
7 R-R1!   K-N6

For, if 7 ... P-N7; 8 RxP, the remaining Pawn is pinned.

8 K-B3   Resigns

Illusion

The following position has all the earmarks of a mopping-up operation. White's Pawns apparently are doomed, for the

White King seems to be too far away to lend support. All is not what it seems!

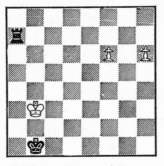

White to Move and Draw

| 1 | K-B4 | . . . . |

Given time, of course, White aims to protect the Pawns.

| 1 | . . . . | R-KB2 |

Soon, it seems, there will be no Pawns. . . .

| 2 | P-R7! | . . . . |

. . . but White has other ideas on the subject.

| 2 | . . . . | RxRP |
| 3 | K-Q5 | . . . . |

White's last Pawn move has sidetracked the Rook just enough to give the King time to defend the remaining Pawn.

Drawn

For after 4 K-K6 and P-B7, the Rook must fall for the Pawn.

Another Illusion

Three Pawns can be mighty dangerous even against a Rook. Here, curiously, even without the assistance of the King, they are self-sustaining.

White to Move and Draw

1 P-K6   R-QB6

The Rook heads for the first rank. For, anywhere else, the Rook cannot inflict any real damage. Thus, if *1* ... R-K6; *2* P-K7. The Pawns then protect themselves, for the Bishop Pawn is immune to capture by the Rook or King, since a capture will allow one of the other Pawns to Queen.

2 K-N5   R-B1
3 K-N6   . . . .

Not now *3* P-K7 because of *4* ... R-K1, followed by ... K-B2 and ... KxP.

3 . . . .   K-R2!

Black threatens *4* ... R-K1, after which Pawns will fall.

4 K-N7   . . . .

It seems that White is too late, but a neat trick turns the tables.

4 . . . .   R-K1
5 P-N8(Q)ch!   . . . .

Not 5 P-K7, K-N1; 6 K-B7, K-B2; 7 K-Q7, R-QR1, as the Pawns then fall.

	5	RxQ

Forced.

	6 P-B7	R-KB1

Otherwise 7 P-K7.

	7 K-B6!	K-N2
	8 P-K7	KxP
	Drawn	

A Flock of Finesses

This Rook versus Pawns ending combines a number of diverse ideas to bring about the final denouement.

White to Move and Win

It is evident that Black threatens to queen the Rook Pawn in two moves. Hence, White must make haste.

1 K-K7 ....

White's strategic plan is to trade off his Rook for the Rook Pawn, providing he can pick off both of Black's remaining Pawns. Then, with his extra Knight Pawn, he hopes to win.

The reason for the original King move is not clear at this juncture. It will become clear, however, as the play progresses.

There are a certain number of finesses based upon the King sortie.

	1	**P-R7**
	2 **K-Q6!**	....

White answers 2 ... P-R8(Q) by 3 RxQ, KxR; 4 KxP, followed by 5 K-B4 and 6 KxP.

	2	**P-K5**
	3 **K-B5!**	....

The oblique movement of the King is the only way, for a reason which is not yet apparent. It does provide at the moment, however, for 3 ... P-R8(Q) by 4 RxQ, KxR; 5 K-Q4 and the mopping up of both remaining Black Pawns.

	3	**P-K6**
	4 **K-N4!!**	....

All part and parcel of the same plan. The King belongs on N4, as will be seen in the next play. Of course if here 4 ... P-R8(Q), White is able to give up the Rook and gain both of Black's other Pawns with an easy win.

	4	**P-K7**

Now for the point. Observe that both of the Kings are in opposition. This allows the following finesse.

	5 **R-K7**	**P-R8(Q)**
	6 **RxPch**	....

Because the Kings are in opposition, the Black King cannot escape. The newly created Queen is forfeit.

	6	**K-N8**
	7 **R-K1ch**	**K-R7**
	8 **RxQch**	**Resigns**

The rest is easy.

15

Know your endings! *Is the position in the photograph above the usual draw of Rook against Bishop? Or can you contrive a win for White? Tackle the problem first. Then see last example, page 151.*

Rook versus Bishop

THERE is a vast difference, according to the table of relative values, between a Rook and a Bishop. A Rook is the equivalent of five Pawns, a Bishop of only three. That is why a Rook and other material will generally prevail over a Bishop and like material with consummate ease.

143

When the position simmers down to a lone Rook versus a lone Bishop, however, that is another story. The result is usually a draw. The manifest injustice of the denouement is only one more example of the absence of complete equity in the game of chess.

The rule of thumb then is that a lone Rook only draws against a lone Bishop. Like all such rules, however, this one, too, is subject to exceptions. By the exceptions shall you know the rule.

THE "OPPOSITION" BROOKS NO OPPOSITION

In lone Rook versus lone Bishop endings the only winning chance arises when the inferior King is on the edge of the board or can be driven to that sector. In all cases the superior King must be in opposition to the other, or must be in position to take the opposition at an opportune moment.

White Wins

This position is a set up.

1	R-R2ch	B-R5
2	R-R1	Resigns

Black must abandon the Bishop.

A MORE PRACTICAL TEST

One of the standard winning positions follows. Here the Black King is in a mating net. No matter how the Bishop squirms, Black will lose.

White Wins

The general plan is to force the Bishop to a poor square, from which point it can be attacked with fatal results.

1 R-QB6   B-Q1

A poor square is Black's B5. Then *2* R-B4, B-K6; *3* R-R4ch, B-R3; *4* R *tempos* on the file, K-R1; *5* RxB mate.

2 R-Q6   B-B2

2 ... B-N4 will not do because of *3* R-Q3. Black then cannot defend against the threat of R-R3ch; for, after *3* ... K-R3, *4* R-R3ch wins, the Bishop serving as a block. Nor is *2* ... B-R4 good because of the reply, *3* R-Q5, attacking the Bishop, followed by *4* R-R5ch, winning. Nor is *2* ... B-R5 good because of *3* R-Q4, attacking the Bishop. If then *3* ... B-N4, *4* R-Q3, as previously, wins. Or, if *3* ... B-N6; *4* R-Q3, B-R5; *5* R-R6, and White wins.

3 R-Q7   B-N3

3 ... B-N1 is also possible. Black is putting up the greatest resistance.

4 **R-N7!**   **B-K6**

On *4* . . . B-Q1 or *4* . . . B-Q3, White wins with *5* K-K8dis.ch or *5* K-K6dis.ch, winning the Bishop.

5 **R-N3**   **Resigns**

For there is nothing to be done against the menacing R-R3(ch).

AN ILLUSION POINTS A RULE

The following position appears to be a win. It is, however, only a draw.

White Draws

Black threatens *1* . . . B-B5ch, which will keep White from maintaining the opposition. For if *2* K-B8, K-R2. Hence, White checks.

1 **R-R2ch**   **B-R2**
Draw

There is no way, with correct play, of making progress. A Rook *tempo* only produces a stalemate.

The rule is that the game is a draw if the inferior King is cornered where the Bishop controls the double corner and the Bishop is able to interpose, or drive the opposing King away.

THE REAL TEST

Where the Kings are in secure opposition, which cannot be disturbed by a Bishop check (as in the previous position), the result is almost always a win. Precision technique, however, is required.

White Wins

With Black to move, the game is a draw. *1* ... K-R4 or *1* ... K-R6 is good enough. But White is on the move.

1 R-R1   B-N7

If *1* ... B-R6; *2* R-R1, Black must abandon his Bishop.

At N7 the Bishop creates a situation on which White must capitalize.

2 R-R5   ....

An important move. This restrains the movement of the Black King. For if now *2* ... K-R6; *3* R-R5 is mate, the Bishop serving as a block.

Hence, the Bishop must move, and there is a way of exploiting each one of its moves.

2 ....   B-B8

The Bishop returns. On other tries, Black also loses: e.g., *2* ... B-R8; *3* R-R3 (preventing a King move), B-N7; *4* R-KN3,

and the Bishop must fall in a few moves. To continue: *4* ...
B-Q4; *5* R-N5, B-B3; *6* R-N6, B-K1; *7* R-R6ch, B-R4; *8* Rook
tempos on the file, King moves *9* RxB, etc.

White is able to trap the Bishop no matter where it goes.
For a good exercise, try the alternate possibilities until you
have full command of what is involved.

3 **R-KN5!**   . . . .

This is a key play. It permits Black momentarily to break
the opposition.

3 . . . .   **K-R6**

Again there are Bishop moves which create problems. There
are, however, solutions to them. For instance, *3* ... B-R6 is
met by *4* R-N8, and the check at R8 is fatal.

Or *3* ... B-Q6; *4* R-N3, B-B5; *5* R-QB3, B-N4 (Black tries
to keep off a poor square which will permit a lateral attack and
a later threat of mate); *6* R-N3, B-B5; *7* R-N4. The Bishop is
lost: *7* ... B-Q4 or *7* ... B-Q6; *8* K-K5dis.ch or *8* K-K3dis.ch,
respectively. Or *7* ... B-K7; *8* R-N2, followed by *9* R-R2ch,
etc. Or *7* ... B-B8; *8* R-N1, B-N7; *9* R-N8, K-R4; *10* R-R8ch,
K-N3; *11* R-N8ch and the Bishop falls.

It is to be noted that, with *7* ... B-B8, the position is nearly
the same one as in the diagram. The main difference is White's
Rook on the Knight file and able to play to N8; whereas, in
the diagrammed position, when Black's Bishop is forced to
Black's N7, White is unable to continue with R-R8, for that
square is controlled by the Bishop.

4 **R-N3ch**   . . . .

This brings the Kings back into opposition or creates a position similar to our second diagram.

4 . . . .   **K-R7**

If *4* ... K-R5, *5* R-N1, B-R6; *6* R-KR1, etc.

5 **K-B3**   **B-K7ch**

A spite check, of no avail.

6 **K-B2**   **Resigns**

No matter where the wicked Bishop may flee, the White Rook pursueth.

EXCEPTION AGAIN!

There is no rule that will cover all positions. Here, for example, the Kings are not in opposition. If White takes the opposition with *1* K-N6, Black breaks it with *1* ... K-B1. Yet, because of the geometric limitations of the Bishop and the board, White wins.

1 **R-Q4!**   . . . .

Black is in *zugzwang*. If he did not have to move, he could draw. But he must move.

1 . . . .   **B-B8**

Clearly *1* ... K-B1 allows mate on the move. *1* ... K-R1 or *1* ... K-R2 allows 2 R-R4ch, winning the Bishop. Bishop to any other square allows an immediate capture of the Bishop or the gain of the Bishop in a move.

2 **K-N6!**   . . . .

Threatening mate, and there is no valid escape.

2 . . . .   **Resigns**

After *2* ... K-B1, *3* R-B4ch wins the Bishop. Since the Bishop cannot break the opposition by a check, Black resigns.

AND AGAIN!

The unhappy situation of the Black Bishop here, too, is enough for Black's downfall.

1 **K-B5** . . . .

Threatening mate.

1 . . . . **K-R3**

There is no Bishop check to break the opposition, and *1* . . . K-R5 loses to *2* R-B4ch.

2 **K-B6** . . . .

Taking the opposition and threatening to win as in the first example.

2 . . . . **K-R4**

Breaking the opposition.

3 **R-B5ch** **K-R3**

Forced, for, after *3* . . . K-R5, *4* R-B4ch wins the Bishop.

4 **R-B4** **Resigns**

The check at R4 is fatal.

FINAL TEST

Often in a Rook and Bishop ending the win is there. But, as Tarrasch has said, "You must see it." To see it, of course, presupposes that you have a fundamental idea of what is involved.

White Wins

1 **R-B3**	. . . .

Threatening mate.

1	**B-Q2**
2 **R-KN3!**	. . . .

The star move. Observe the various moves at Black's command. *1* . . . B-B1 loses the Bishop to a check. Other Bishop moves leave the Bishop subject to capture, except *2* . . . B-B4.

2	**K-R2**

If *2* . . . B-B4; *3* R-N8ch, K-R2; *4* R-N5, and White wins the Bishop.

3 **R-N5**	. . . .

Threatening mate.

3 ....   **K-R3**

To break the opposition.

4 **K-B6**   **Resigns**

Taking the opposition and reaching the standard position. Black may not break the opposition by *4* ... K-R2 on account of *5* R-N7ch, winning the Bishop.

16

Know your endings! *How does White win here? Don't let
preconceived notions influence you here. Solve the problem on
your own merits. Can you? For answer, see last example.*

Rook and Pawn versus Rook

IT IS NOT so strange that many epic battles of the chessboard
culminate in an ending with a Pawn plus for one of the players.
It is, indeed, a likelihood that a game between more or less
evenly matched adversaries in a contest of attrition will pro-
duce such an insignificant difference. When that extra Pawn is
in a position which has simmered down to Rook and Pawn
play, as is often the case, the result is problematical. There are
times when the Pawn wins perforce, and there are times when
the Pawn can be checked.

To distinguish between the resulting wins and draws demands a refined technique. In some cases, for example, the only drawing method is to bring the Rook behind the Pawn. In other cases, the only method is to bring the Rook to the side or in front of the Pawn. To know these ideas is the certain path to correct planning and projecting in Rook and Pawn endings.

A BASIC EXAMPLE

With a Pawn behind here, White can hold the game even.

White Draws

Because White is a Pawn behind, the onus of proving the draw rests with him. From the diagrammed position many moves, if correctly pursued, will draw. There is, however, one principle that embraces the correct technique. It involves the defense on the third rank. Black's King shall not cross onto White's third rank.

1 **R-KN3** . . . .

For all intents and purposes, a stall. White bides his time until Black threatens to enter White's third rank.

1 . . . . **R-R7ch**

Black drives the enemy King to the first rank.

2 **K-K1** . . . .

2 K-Q1 is just as good.

2 . . . . **K-Q4**

Black's plan is to play 3 ... K-B5, followed by ... P-Q6 and ... K-B6, when the concerted action of all his forces will smooth the path of the Pawn to the eighth.

3 **K-Q1**   . . . .

White stalls again. His stand is on the third rank.

3 . . . .   **K-B5**

4 **R-KR3**   . . . .

Still biding his time, White holds the third rank.

4 . . . .   **P-Q6**

Now Black threatens ... K-B6. The time has come for counter-action.

5 **R-R8!**   . . . .

White dare not permit the Black King to reach B6 unmolested.

Why did White select this particular moment to go to R8? The reason is simple and clear. Heretofore, a Rook move to the eighth allowed the Black King to go to B6, after which a Rook check from behind would have driven the King to Q6, where it would have been sheltered. Black would then have been in a winning position. Since Black's Pawn moved to Q6, however, the Pawn no longer can afford shelter to the King. Hence, the timing of the Rook move.

Draw

No matter how Black plays, he is subject to flailing checks, which he cannot very well avoid. A Rook interposition, for example, permits the exchange of Rooks and a subsequent draw.

Before examining the next position, let us summarize the salient features of the drawing method.

(1) White maintains his Rook on the third rank, preventing the Black King from crossing onto that rank.

(2) When the Black King threatens to invade, White essays his Rook to the eighth, and Black cannot successfully ward off the ensuing checks.

Worthy of note is that this ending is basic. The same method applies if Black's Pawn is on some other file or rank. Then White takes his stand on another rank, never permitting the Black King shelter in front of the Pawn.

AN UNLIKE PAIR OF EXAMPLES

With the Pawn advanced to the sixth rank, as in the following position, and the superior King sheltered from molesting checks, the result is usually a win for the Pawn. Here it does not matter who moves first, White wins.

White Wins

1 **R-KR2** . . . .

White threatens mate. With Black on the move, the result is the same, since his Rook is tied to the first rank to prevent mate.

	1	....	**K-N1**
	2	**R-N2ch**	**K-R2**

If 2 ... K-B1; 3 P-K7ch, followed by 4 R-N8ch, decides.

	3	**K-B7**	**Resigns**

There is nought can be done about both the threat of R-R2 mate and that of the advance of the Pawn simultaneously.

In many respects the following position is similar to the previous one. There is, however, one vital difference—the Pawn is on the Knight file. Because of that factor, the position is a draw.

	1	....	**R-R7**
	2	**R-QB1**	....

Or any other move with the Rook on the first rank.

	2	....	**R-N7ch**
	3	**K-R1**	....

Not 3 K-B1, for then ... K-R7 wins.

3	....	**R-R7ch**
4	**K-N1**	....
	Draw	

Black can make no further progress. He must not advance ... P-N7 on account of 5 R-B3ch.

THE LUCENA POSITION

When, as in the following diagram, the inferior King is cut off from the defense, the Pawn generally wins. The winning technique, however, is a matter of knowledge.

White Wins

1	....	**R-Q8**

There is no valid defense for Black, but he can put up strong resistance. The text move offers the best chances.

2	**K-B5**	....

White makes way for the advance of the Pawn.

2	....	**R-B8ch**
3	**K-Q6**	....

Thereby White leaves the square, Q5, vacant, so that the Pawn can advance.

3	....	R-Q8
4	P-Q5	R-Q6

Black can do no better than stall.

5	K-B6	R-B6ch
6	K-Q7	....

Again White leaves Q6 vacant for the advance of the Pawn.

6	....	R-Q6
7	P-Q6	R-Q8
8	K-B7	R-B8ch
9	K-Q8	R-Q8

So far so good. White has made progress in getting the Pawn down. Following the next move, White's play will require a new plan.

10	P-Q7	R-QB8

Now, how does White extricate his King and succeed in queening his Pawn?

11	R-B2ch	....

The first of the important moves. The Black King must be driven away from guarding the exit.

11	....	K-N2
12	R-B5!	....

A star move. White can make no progress by exiting with his King to K7, thus: *12* K-K7, R-K8ch; *13* K-Q6, R-Q8ch; *14* K-B7, R-B8ch; *15* K-Q8, R-QB8.

After the text move, White does threaten to exit with his King. For, assuming it is White's move, *13* K-K7, R-K8ch; *14* K-Q6, R-Q8ch; *15* R-Q5, and it is over. The Rook, by going to the fifth rank, is preparing to interpose on one of the checks.

12	....	K-N3
13	R-B4	....

13 K-K7 works also by tricky play. It resolves the ending, however, into a Queen versus Rook ending. And it is not the thematic continuation.

Now White threatens to bring his King out, and, after exhausting Black's checks, interpose his Rook at either K4 or Q4 and so cut off Black's Rook from the action on the Pawn.

13	. . . .	**K-N2**

If *13* ... K-N4; *14* R-B7 and the threat of *15* K-K8, followed by queening of the Pawn, cannot be met.

14	**K-K7**	**R-K8ch**
15	**K-Q6**	**R-Q8ch**
16	**K-K6**	**R-K8ch**

Otherwise *17* R-B5-Q5. If *16* ... K-N3, *17* R-B8 and the Pawn cannot be stopped.

17	**K-Q5**	**R-Q8ch**
18	**R-Q4**	**Resigns**

THE ROOK PAWN EXCEPTION

In almost every phase of the ending, the Rook Pawn plays its exceptional part. With Rooks on the board, the Rook Pawn, too, voids all preconceived principles.

Here is one of the important exceptions. The Black King is ahead of its Pawn and the White King is cut off from participation in the critical sector. Yet the result is a draw.

Draw

Despite the advantage in Black's favor, there is little he can do. For, on the edge of the board, the Black King is limited in scope. There is only one try: It is to bring the Black Rook to Black's KN6, N7, or N8. When the Rooks are opposed, the White Rook will be compelled to abandon the file. Then, maybe, the Black King will exit.

| 1 | .... | R-QR2 |
| 2 | K-K2 | .... |

White must anticipate Black's action. If he merely temporizes, he will lose. He must bring his King, at the first opportunity, to KB1 or KB2.

| 2 | .... | R-R7ch |
| 3 | K-B1 | R-KN7 |

Now the Rooks are opposed, and White must abandon the Knight file.

| 4 | R-KB8 | .... |

There are many moves that are sufficient here. The text move is made with a view to preclude Black from checking on the Bishop file later on, and driving off the White King.

| 4 | .... | K-N6 |

The King is out. But not for long.

| 5 | R-N8ch | K-R7 |

The King popped out but has nowhere to go. On other moves, such as ... K-B6 or K-R5, the Rook checks relentlessly until such time as the King abandons the Pawn. Then the Rook attacks the Rook Pawn, and Black is unable to make progress.

6 R-KB8   **Draw**

If Black continues with ... K-R8 and ... P-R7, he is unable to exit with his King.

THE EXCEPTION EXCEPTED

The following position has all the earmarks of the previous one with a vital difference. That difference, however, is enough to turn the usual draw into a win for White.

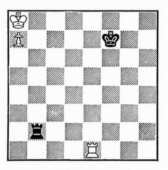

White Wins

The Black King is now limited to the Bishop file. This factor gives White ample time to describe the winning maneuver.

1 R-KR1   . . . .

The plan is to bring the Rook to QN8 as quickly as possible.

1 . . . .   **K-K2**

As before, Black hurries to post his King on ... QB1 or ... QB2.

2 R-R8   **K-Q2**

3 R-QN8   . . . .

Now Black must abandon the file, while White has an exit for his King.

	3	**R-QB7**
	4 **K-N7**	. . . .

White threatens to queen.

	4	**R-N7ch**
	5 **K-R6**	**R-R7ch**
	6 **K-N6**	**R-N7ch**
	7 **K-B5!**	. . . .

White queens perforce.

It is to be noted that, had Black played his King to Q3 to guard the exit at White's B5, White would still have won by playing his King to B8.

	7	**Resigns**

ROOK TO THE FORE!

Generally speaking, the Rook is most effective behind the Pawn. There are times, however, when the vantage point is in front of the Pawn. Here is an instance.

Draw

White has much in his favor here. He is not only a Pawn to the good but also the Black King is shut out of the defense.

Yet Black's King and Rook are sufficiently disposed to hold matters even.

1 **K-B4**   . . . .

Or *1* K-R4, R-R1ch; *2* K-N5, R-N1ch; *3* K-B4, reaching the text position.

1 . . . .   **R-KR1**

Now White is at a loss to make progress. If his Rook moves, then *2* . . . K-B3, after which Black's King joins the defense, and Black draws as in "A Basic Example." White dare not advance his Pawn on account of *2* . . . R-R5ch, after which White's Rook is vulnerable. Hence, White is reduced to temporizing or taking a stand on a slim prospect.

2 **K-N3**   . . . .

White returns, hoping that Black may go wrong.

2 . . . .   **R-QN1**

As good as any. But not, for example, . . . R-R8 with the idea of getting behind the Pawn, for then *3* R-B3 gives White the necessary setup to be able to advance his Pawn to N5.

3 **K-R4**   **R-R1ch**
4 **R-R5**   **R-R1**

Of course not the exchange of Rooks.

5 **K-N5**   **R-N1ch**
6 **K-B4**   **R-B1ch**
7 **R-B5**   . . . .

White can make no headway.

7 . . . .   **RxRch**
8 **PxRch**   **K-B3**
Draw

ILLUSION!

According to all the rules and regulations, the following position ought to be an easy win for White. It isn't.

Everything is favorable for White here. He is a Pawn to the good; his King is in front of the Pawn; and the queening path is clear. Yet Black can hold the game.

1 .... **R-N3!**

The star move. What is White to do? His King cannot move without giving up the Pawn, and on R-K7, Black temporizes.

2 **P-K7** ....

The only attempt at progress. 2 R-KR8 avails nothing: *2* ... RxP; *3* R-R5ch, K-N4; *4* KxR, KxR.

2 .... **R-B3ch**
3 **K-N7** **R-N3ch**
4 **K-R7** ....

If *4* K-R8, R-R3.

With White out of check at last it now appears that Black is doomed.

4 .... **K-B3!**

Black must win the Pawn.

5 **R-B8ch** . . . .

On most other Rook moves there follows ... R-N2ch, and the gain of the Pawn.

5 . . . . **KxP**
Draw

Each Rook is *en prise*.

17

Know your endings! *Black on the move can draw in the above position. White on the move wins. There is a problem involved which is well worth knowing. The principle is easy; the practical discovery of the best move may not be.*

Queen versus Pawn

THE DIFFERENCE in value between a Queen and a Pawn is so ridiculously great that it seems a discussion on the subject hardly warrants the expenditure of good space, time, and effort. As for so many apparent contradictions, however, there is, indeed, room for elaboration.

When a Pawn reaches the eighth rank, it can be converted into equal force, an opposing Queen. This ever-menacing threat to equalize the game crops up so often in this type of ending that it is imperative to know the technical procedure in winning positions. And, as we have seen so often in study of the end game, the technical procedure involves both general rules, exceptions, and even exceptions to the exceptions. Hence, even this chapter has its special significance.

GENERAL RULE 1

A Pawn even as far as the sixth rank always loses to a Queen except when of course the Queen is subject to immediate capture or when the Pawn can immediately reach the seventh rank and achieve a special drawing position.

White Wins

The goal here is the capture of the Pawn. The procedure calls for concerted action by Queen and King.

1 **Q-B3** . . . .

There are any number of ways of beginning this position. *1* Q-Q6ch, *1* Q-B5ch or even *1* K-B5, are sufficient for examples. White's aim is to compel Black's King to assume a post immediately in front of the Pawn. Then, when the Pawn cannot advance, White's King gains time to approach, eventually to pick off the Pawn or incidentally to checkmate.

1 . . . . **K-Q7**

Black's choice is limited. If he abandons the Pawn, he loses at once. To defend it, he must play the text or *1* . . . K-Q5. The latter will not do because, once the White Queen assumes a post in front of the Pawn, White's task is easy. He approaches with his King and drives the Black King away from the defense of the Pawn.

2 **Q-B4!**   . . . .

Here again White has a vast choice of moves. The text move, however, restricts the Black King more than any other.

2 . . . .   **K-Q6**

Black must abandon the Pawn, get in front of it, or play the text move. Each is equally futile. If *2* . . . K-K7, the White King closes in with *3* K-B5.

3 **K-B5!**   . . . .

This play seems to be out of context, yet it is very strong. Observe that Black must return with his King. For *3* . . . P-K7; *4* Q-QB1, followed by *5* Q-K1, leaves the White Queen in front of the Pawn, and the rest is merely a matter of closing in and mopping up.

3 . . . .   **K-Q7**

4 **K-Q4**   **Resigns**

The Pawn falls.

Observe, too, that the strongest move in the initial position is really *1* Q-B4. After that move, Black may not advance his Pawn because of *2* Q-QB1, and his King can only shuttle back and forth, around the Pawn, until it is forced to abandon it.

A RULE AND AN EXCEPTION

When a Pawn is on the seventh rank, opposing a Queen, the winning procedure is exactly the same as if it were on the sixth or any other rank. The plan is to force the inferior King in front of the Pawn and then to close in with the superior King.

There are, however, a number of exceptions to the general rule. The first exception is that of a Pawn on the seventh which is a Bishop Pawn.

White Draws

The Bishop Pawn makes all the difference. With Black to move, he can make no progress.

1	**Q-N3ch**
2 **K-R8!**	....

We immediately get to the crux of the situation. If the Pawn is a King or Queen Pawn, White cannot afford to abandon the Pawn. Here, however, the Pawn can be left *en prise*. For, on *2* ... QxP, the result is stalemate. Black can make no progress.

2 ....   **Drawn**

EXCEPTION TO THE EXCEPTION

White Wins

With the superior King in bounds, in this case able to reach N3, White can yet win.

1 K-B4!   . . . .

Right into the adverse check!

1 . . . .   K-R1

If *1* ... P-B8ch; 2 K-N3, Black cannot avoid being mated. The text move, however, is a trap, so to speak, Black's last gasp.

2 Q-Q2   . . . .

Of course not 2 QxP stalemate. But also, of course, not 2 K-N3 on account of *2* ... P-B8(N)ch, forking King and Queen.

2 . . . .   K-N7

To hold the Pawn, to hold off White's King and to give White the opportunity to blunder.

3 K-N4   K-N8
4 K-N3   Resigns

For, on *4* ... P-B8(Q), 5 Q-R2 mate. Or, on *4* ... P-B8(N)ch; 5 K-R3, the Knight goes lost.

THE ROOK PAWN EXCEPTION

Whenever there are exceptions to a general rule, it is a sure thing that the Rook Pawn will play a role in them. Here is a case in point.

White Draws

The great disparity of material means nothing here, even with Black to move. The edge of the board favors White.

1	....	**Q-N3ch**
2	**K-R8**	....

Usually, when the King plays in front of the Pawn, the adverse King has an opportunity to inch in. Here, however, no such opportunity exists. For on 2 ... K-K4 the result is stalemate. Black can make no progress.

Drawn

A PARADOX

It is not often that an extra Pawn is a liability. Here it is a distinct one.

White Wins

This position, in most respects, is similar to the previous one, except that Black has an extra Pawn. Curiously, this works to Black's disadvantage. It is truly an exception to the exception.

> *1* **Q-N3ch**   **K-R8**

Black cannot afford to abandon the Pawn.

> *2* **Q-B2**   . . . .

Because Black has a move, White can temporize.

> *2* **P-R5**
> *3* **Q-B1 mate**

A MASQUED BATTERY

There is another case of the exception to the exception. With a Rook Pawn on the seventh rank, the Queen will win if its King can assist in setting up a mating net.

White Wins

1 K-N6 . . . .

By masking the Queen, the King is able to approach the sector of the enemy King.

1	. . . .	**K-N7**
2	**K-B5dis.ch**	**K-B7**

Or 2 . . . K-R8; 3 K-N4, K-N7; 4 Q-R2ch, K-N8; 5 K-N3, etc.

3	**Q-K5**	**K-N8**
4	**Q-K1ch**	**K-N7**
5	**Q-Q2ch**	**K-N8**

Of course not 5 . . . K-R6 or 5 . . . K-N6. Then follows 6 Q-B1, and the Black Pawn falls in short order.

6	**K-N4**	**P-R8(Q)**
7	**K-N3**	**Resigns**

Black cannot avoid mate.

Except for the previous text position, where the White King is able to use the position of the Queen as a maneuvering point for approach to the Black King, the superior side will win when the King is within the bounds outlined on the following diagram.

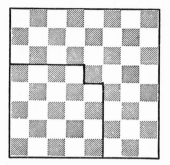

It is to be noted that each square is within two squares of striking distance of either KN3 or KB2. When the King is able to reach either of these two squares within two moves, a mating net can be set up.

RULE 1 AGAIN

When a Pawn is on the sixth rank, as previously stated, it loses to a Queen, unless the Pawn can move at once to the seventh and reach an exceptional position.

The following position, which is a prelude to the next one, is a case in point.

White Wins

1 **Q-N7** . . . .

The thematic move. Whenever the Queen is able to pin the Pawn on the sixth, the rest of the play is simple.

1	K-N7
2 K-K6	....

The White King approaches. Black is at a loss for a continuation.

2	K-N6

Black's choice is limited. He may go to N6 or B7. In either case, he does not threaten to advance his Pawn. And, in each case, the White King closes in.

3 K-Q5	P-B7

Black takes his stand. Otherwise after 3 ... K-B7, White plays 4 K-B4, and it is over.

4 Q-R1	Resigns

It is only a question of a few moves before the Pawn falls.

QUEEN VERSUS BISHOP PAWN

A Pawn on the sixth rank generally loses, as noted above. Sometimes, however, the win is difficult, as in the following position.

White Wins

With Black to move, there is no problem. Black plays ...
P-B7 and secures a draw. With White to move, however, there
is a problem. It stems from the fact that White is unable to
play his Queen onto the long diagonal on the first move
(Q-N7), because the White King is inopportunely posted. And
White is unable successfully to maneuver his Queen to the long
diagonal. Yet there is a way.

Because this position embraces all the ideas of Queen versus
Bishop Pawn, it belongs in the repertoire of all aspiring chess
players. The actual win is easy. To understand all the ideas
which this position embraces, however, is quite a task.

1 Q-R1ch?   . . . .

This is not the best move. In fact, from here on, with best
play, the position is a draw. It is, however, the most likely try.
It is essential for the student to understand why the try will
not work before he can understand fully the thoughts involved
in the position.

1 . . . .   K-N7!

1 ... K-R7 loses quickly. White follows with 2 Q-Q5ch, and
no matter how Black plays, White will be able to pin the Black
Pawn on the diagonal.

2 Q-N7ch   . . . .

Otherwise, 2 ... P-B7 draws.

2 . . . .   K-B8!

The first of a series of star moves. On any other move, White
is able to maneuver into a diagonal pin of the Pawn: e.g.,
2 ... K-R8; *3* Q-R6ch, K-N8; *4* Q-B1ch, K-N7; *5* Q-B6, pinning
the Pawn for an easy win.

The position still offers many hurdles for Black.

3 K-B6!   . . . .

Already having misplayed the position, White pursues his best chance. On other moves (except the repetition of checks) Black advances his Pawn. Then, because the Bishop Pawn reaches the seventh, and because the White King is out of bounds, Black draws. The text move is an attempt to bring the King within bounds.

$$3 \ldots \ldots \qquad \textbf{P-B7}$$
$$4 \ \textbf{K-K5} \qquad \ldots \ldots$$

Still approaching in an effort to bring the King within bounds.

$$4 \ldots \ldots \qquad \textbf{K-Q7}$$

Now Black threatens to Queen.

$$5 \ \textbf{Q-Q5ch!!} \qquad \ldots \ldots$$

Black has five different replies. Four of them lose, one draws.

$$5 \ldots \ldots \qquad \textbf{K-K8!}$$

The drawing move.

5 ... K-B6 loses to 6 Q-Q4ch, followed by 7 Q-R1 and 8 Q-QB1.

5 ... K-B1 loses after 6 Q-R2, K-Q7; 7 K-Q4, K-Q8; 8 K-B3! P-B8(Q)ch; 9 K-Q3 as Black cannot avoid mate.

5 ... K-K7 loses in the same fashion. 6 Q-R2, K-Q6; 7 Q-N2, K-Q7; 8 K-Q4, K-Q8; 9 K-Q3, P-B8(Q); 10 Q-K2 mate. In this line, if 6 ... K-Q7 (instead of 6 ... K-Q6); 7 K-Q4, K-Q8; 8 K-B3, P-B8(Q)ch; 9 K-Q3 and mate soon.

5 ... K-K6 loses to a sharp retort. 6 Q-N2! P-B8(Q); 7 Q-N5ch, followed by picking off the Queen. In this line, if 6 ... K-Q6, then 7 Q-N5, followed by Q-B1, suffices.

$$6 \ \textbf{Q-R5ch} \qquad \ldots \ldots$$

White has not yet given up hope. There is still room for blunder.

> 6 .... **K-Q8**

6 ... K-K7 loses to 7 Q-R2, as previously demonstrated.

> 7 **Q-R4** **K-Q7**

7 ... K-B8 loses to 8 K-Q4, as previously demonstrated.

> 8 **Q-R2** ....

It appears now that White will win, for the position is similar to the winning ones of the previous variations. But there is a difference. Black's King is on Q7, instead of K7. Hence, there is a saving clause.

> 8 .... **K-B6!!**
> **Drawn**

White can make no progress. Thus, 9 Q-R3ch, K-Q7. Now 10 Q-R2, K-B6, repeats the position. And, if 10 Q-N2, K-Q8. White's Queen is on N2 instead of R2, and this slight distinction makes for the draw.

If all of the foregoing leads to a draw with best play, how does White win? That is the problem.

> 1 **Q-R6!!!** **Resigns**

For Black dare not advance his Pawn to B7 on account of 2 Q-B1ch, capturing the Pawn on the following move. If Black fails to advance his Pawn, White is able to maneuver his Queen into a position where he pins the Pawn on the diagonal, and the rest is easy.

18

*****

End Games — Max Euwe

FROM time to time we have stressed the point that theoretical
knowledge is of little value without practical application. The
theorist usually wins the "post mortems," while the practical
player wins the games.

The following section, contributed by former world champion, Dr. Max Euwe, is all on the practical side. It comprises
a selection of end games culled mostly from practical play
among the experts and masters. It will give the learner a small
idea of the problems confronting the over-the-board player in
converting theory into practice.

KINGS AND PAWNS

In the course of Dr. Euwe's main thesis, the difference
between composed endings and end games from actual play,
he demonstrates some particularly fine points about King and

Pawn end games and the related King and Queen versus King, Queen, and Pawn end games. The one special finesse involves a surprise sacrifice of a Pawn to prevent a winning liquidation (exchange of Queens, reducing to King versus King and Pawn).

On the whole, however, the main lesson may be in the value of probing apparently simple positions deeply enough to uncover the great number of hidden, winning, or drawing finesses which actually often do exist.

We start off with an end-game composition by the famous Pawn artist N. D. Grigoriev.

White to Play and Win

This end game shows once more what finesses lie concealed behind seemingly simple positions, and it demonstrates especially the great number of facets in an end game of such limited material.

1 P-N4!   ....

First of all, it is evident that, after *1* ... PxP; *2* P-R5, White wins as his Pawn queens with check. Black's passed Pawns, true enough, are as far advanced as the White one; but, even so, Black must lose an extra *tempo* to get one of his through: *2* ... P-N6; *3* P-R6, P-N7; *4* K-B2, P-B6; *5* P-R7, P-B7; *6* P-R8(Q)ch, etc.

| 1 .... | K-K2 |
| 2 P-N5 | .... |

Clearly White's only move as, after 2 PxP, K-Q2, the Black King has entered within the Pawn's "square."

| 2 .... | K-Q3 |

Seemingly the end of the fun. White has a protected, passed Pawn which ties up Black's King so his own King can go undisturbedly after Black's Bishop Pawn.

| 3 K-K2 | K-K3 |
| 4 K-B3 | K-K4 |

Black's King just barely guards the Bishop Pawn without quitting the square of White's passed Pawn. If it were now Black's move, his King would be committed to a choice of going after that Knight Pawn fruitlessly or leaving its square, to hold the Bishop Pawn, equally fruitlessly. From White's point of view, therefore, it obviously now becomes a matter of gaining a *tempo* (or losing one) by means of "triangulation." Not so; Black's King neatly copies all of White's King figures: e.g., 5 K-B2, K-K3; 6 K-K2, K-Q3; 7 K-Q3, K-Q4; 8 K-K2, K-Q3; 9 K-Q2, K-K3, etc.

So White has but one try left.

5 K-N4   K-K5

Now Black's King, it is true, has quit the "square," so White's Pawn can advance to queen. But then so can Black's.

6 P-N6   P-B6
7 K-N3   K-K6

The interpolation of these two King moves is of no importance whatever to the Pawn ending; but it is of decisive significance with regard to the coming Queen end game.

8 P-N7   P-B7
9 P-N8(Q)   P-B8(Q)

Believe it or not, White now wins by force!

10 Q-K5ch   K-Q7

Not 10 ... K-Q6?? 11 Q-N5ch.

11 QxPch   K-Q8

Other possibilities are: (1) 11 ... K-K6; 12 Q-K5ch, K-Q7; 13 Q-B4ch, etc. (2) 11 ... K-B7 (or K-B8); 12 Q-QB5ch, K-N6 (or 7 or 8); 13 Q-N5ch, etc.—or 12 ... K-Q7; 13 Q-KB2ch, etc.

—or *12* ... K-Q8; *13* Q-Q4ch, K-B7; *14* Q-B2ch or *13* ... K-B8; *14* Q-R1ch.

12 Q-Q5ch   K-K8

On *12* ... K-B8; *13* Q-B5ch, we arrive at the variations in the preceding note.

13 Q-K4ch   ....

And White wins after *13* ... K-Q8; *14* Q-N1ch or *13* ... K-Q7; *14* Q-N2ch.

Splendid work, but a composition remains a composition. We have a feeling that this and similar surprising developments would, in practice, occur only by high exception. So we can value the composed end game as an expression of art but must deny it any practical significance.

One who examines end games regularly, however, and who thus often makes surprising discoveries rather inclines to the conclusion that the beautiful windings actually do lie concealed in most practical end games but are usually missed because they are too deeply hidden.

For example, here is the position from a game played in the latest Marshall Chess Club championship in New York City. It makes a remarkable comparison with the Grigoriev composition.

Allen Kaufman

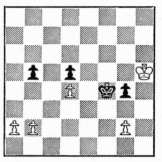

Frank Howard

It is Black's move. After some concentration on this position, the issues are seemingly rather simple. The Black King will proceed to capture the Queen Pawn—whether voluntarily or by compulsion—White takes the Knight Pawn, the two passed Pawns advance, both sides queen their Pawns, and a draw becomes the likely result.

Let us convert this idea into a variation.

(1) *1* ... K-K5; *2* KxP, KxP; *3* K-B4, K-Q6; *4* P-KN4, P-Q5; *5* P-N5, K-B7; *6* P-N6, P-Q6; *7* P-N7, P-Q7; *8* P-N8(Q), P-Q8(Q).

Halt! Here already is our first "point": with *9* Q-N3ch, White exchanges Queens and wins the Pawn ending (*9* ... K-B8; *10* QxQch, KxQ; *11* P-N3! P-N5; *12* K-K4, K-B7; *13* K-Q4, K-N7; *14* K-B4, etc.). This last phase must still be carefully managed, but it all proves to work out right.

Hence, Black's King seems to have moved to an unfortunate square. Black could have tried *5* ... K-K7, instead of *5* ... K-B7. But then, too, things go amiss with Black: *6* P-N6, P-Q6; *7* P-N7, P-Q7; *8* P-N8(Q), P-Q8(Q); *9* Q-N4ch, with the same consequences as before.

Rather nice, but commonplace even so. These developments present about the highest we can expect from actual practice: the side first to promote then forces the exchange of Queens and wins the resulting Pawn ending.

But we have not finished yet. These two pretty but somewhat trite checks are the forerunners of a series of finesses.

But first let us demonstrate that a number of other initial moves but lead to a loss for Black:

(2) *1* ... K-N6? *2* K-N5, KxP; *3* KxP, and White wins easily with no real problems whatsoever.

(3) *1* ... P-N5; *2* P-R4, PxP e.p.; *3* PxP, K-K5; *4* P-R4, KxP; *5* P-R5, K-B4; *6* KxP, K-N4 (or *6* ... P-Q5; *7* P-R6); *7* K-B4, and White captures the Queen Pawn and wins with his Knight Pawn.

(4) *1* ... P-N6; *2* K-R4, K-K5; *3* KxP, KxP; *4* K-B4 leads to

our first variation, whereas *2* ... P-N5; *3* P-R4, PxP e.p.; *4* PxP comes to about the same as our last.

As yet there is still no special finesse in sight. We do observe one if we continue incorrectly for White:

(5) *1* ... P-N5; *2* K-R4? K-K5; *3* KxP, KxP; *4* K-B4 (let us observe, in passing, that, after *4* K-B5, K-K6, Black queens first and, after *4* K-B3? K-Q6, Black subsequently queens with check), K-Q6; *5* P-N4, P-Q5; *6* P-N5, K-B7; *7* P-N6 (so far, all quite ordinary, but now comes the finesse), P-N6!!

Now, after *8* PxP, P-Q6; *9* P-N7, P-Q7; *10* P-N8(Q), P-Q8-(Q), White has lost his chance to check (*11* Q-N3ch, comparable to *9* Q-N3ch in our first variation, is impossible here), and Black achieves a draw without too much difficulty.

So now let us start over, and make use of the development just shown, without White's making an error.

(Start from diagram labeled Howard—Kaufman)

1	K-K5
2 KxP	P-N5!

Black's last is a venomous move. If White now plays *3* K-N3, Black attains the draw in the manner indicated above: *3* ... KxP; *4* K-B4 (or *4* K-B2), K-Q6; *5* P-N4, P-Q5; *6* P-N5, P-N6!

3 P-R4!	PxP e.p.
4 PxP	KxP

5 P-R4   . . . .

Again a difficult situation has come up. It is typical of this sort of end game in which both sides are threatening to queen.

If Black's King now disposes of the Rook Pawn, he loses his own passed Pawn, whereby Black's fate is settled, of course: e.g., 5 ... K-B4; 6 P-R5, K-N4; 7 K-B4, etc.

Consequently, Black must let it come down to a race and move his King in such manner as not to hinder the advance of his Pawn. 5 ... K-K6 is obvious, but the sequel leads to a disappointing outcome: 6 P-R5, P-Q5; 7 P-R6, P-Q6; 8 P-R7, P-Q7; 9 P-R8(Q), P-Q8(Q)ch; 10 Q-B3ch! The same cross check by White is conclusive after 5 ... K-B6; 6 P-R5, P-Q5; 7 P-R6, P-Q6; 8 P-R7, P-Q7; 9 P-R8(Q), P-Q8(Q)ch; 10 Q-B3ch!

At his wit's end, Black has a try with the correct move.

5 . . . .   K-B5!

One is inclined at first to reject this move also, as White's King can now return—but this is an illusion: 6 K-B3, K-B6! For now Black is exempt from that murderous cross-check on White's KB3, and he is safe enough with either 7 P-R5, P-Q5; 8 P-R6, P-Q6 after which he queens with no difficulties or

7 K-K2, K-B7; 8 K-K3, K-B6 which presents no new viewpoints. Hence, White's King cannot return. The race is unavoidable.

6 P-R5	P-Q5	9 P-R8(Q)	P-Q8(Q)ch
7 P-R6	P-Q6	10 Q-B3	....
8 P-R7	P-Q7		

Although it is true that this interposition does not take place with check, it is nevertheless very useful. The White Queen guards its King against perpetual check, and so White's Pawn plus begins to matter.

Also, now with Black's King much less favorably posted, there is constant danger of an exchange of Queens, and one may suppose that this Queen ending is, in the long run, won for White: e.g., 10 ... Q-Q2ch; 11 Q-B5, Q-N2ch; 12 Q-N5, Q-Q2ch; 13 K-R4, Q-R2ch; 14 Q-R5, Q-K2ch; 15 K-R3, Q-K6ch; 16 P-N3, Q-N8; 17 Q-K5, Q-R8ch; 18 K-N4, Q-Q8ch; 19 K-R4, Q-R8ch; 20 K-N5, and White always progresses, slowly, very slowly, but steadily.

The last variation may not rank as proof that White has a forced win; but there is, nevertheless, occasion for Black to try to find a continuation which may perhaps offer better drawing chances. And such a continuation, indeed, proves to be present.

Let us start over again.

(Start from diagram labeled Howard—Kaufman)

1 ....   K-B4!

Now White can choose between the following, vainly:

(1) 2 P-R3, K-K5! 3 KxP, KxP; 4 K-B4, K-Q6; 5 P-KN4, P-Q5; 6 P-N5, K-B7; 7 P-N6, P-Q6; 8 P-N7, P-Q7; 9 P-N8(Q), P-Q8(Q), and here White lacks that winning check, with Q-QN3;

(2) 2 P-QN3 (or P-QN4) yields even less: 2 ... K-K5; 3 KxP, KxP; 4 K-B4, and Black has the important *tempo*, 4 ... K-B6! following which he is in no danger of losing;

(3) 2 K-R4, K-B5, and White gets no further, since the moves, 3 P-R3, 3 P-QN3, and 3 P-QN4, lead into the above variations, while 3 P-N3ch, K-K5 transposes into the following variation.

White, therefore, has only the following text.

2 P-KN3 ....

This move forces Black's King to give ground, and we again arrive on familiar terrain.

2 .... K-K5

After 2 ... P-N5; 3 P-R4, PxP e.p.; 4 PxP, K-K5; 5 P-R4, White wins easily as previously demonstrated.

3 KxP P-N5!

Now this finesse again. As we know from previous discussion, Black manages nicely on 4 K-N5, KxP; 5 K-B4, K-Q6; 6 P-N4, P-Q5; 7 P-N5, P-N6! 8 PxP, K-B7, etc.

4 P-R4	PxP e.p.	
5 PxP	KxP	
6 P-R4	....	

After 6 K-B3, K-B6, White can only force a draw by repetition of moves: 7 K-K2, K-B7; 8 K-K3, K-B6 (9 P-R5 permits

Black's Pawn to go through, queening first by gain of *tempo* from 9 ... P-Q5ch).

Now we have the same situation as diagrammed earlier, except that White's King Knight Pawn stands on N3 instead of N2, an important difference!

6	K-K6!	9 P-R7	P-Q7
7 P-R5	P-Q5	10 P-R8(Q)	P-Q8(Q)ch
8 P-R6	P-Q6		

Thus here (without the Pawn on N2) White lacks the cross-check at KB3. Also, in other respects this Queen ending is significantly better for Black than the one in the previous diagram.

The following variations tend to demonstrate that Black obtains a draw:

(1) *11* K-N5, Q-Q3! *12* P-N4, Q-K4ch; *13* K-R6, Q-K3ch; *14* K-R5, Q-B2ch; *15* K-R4, Q-B7ch; *16* K-R3, Q-B8ch; *17* Q-N2, QxQch; *18* KxQ, K-B5;

(2) *11* K-R4, Q-Q5ch; *12* P-N4, Q-B3ch; *13* P-N5, Q-B5ch; *14* K-R5, Q-R7ch; *15* K-N6, Q-Q3ch; *16* K-N7 (*16* K-B7, Q-B5ch), K-B5; *17* P-N6, Q-Q2ch; *18* K-N8, K-N4; *19* P-N7, Q-K3ch, etc.

The comparison of these two end games demonstrates the difference between composition and practice. The composed end game is a finished product in all variations, the practical end game still raises doubts at some points. Is the next to the last diagram indeed a win? Is the last indeed a draw?

Therein lies the difference between composition and practice, not in the presence of surprise turns, because those are to be found in the practical game as well, if one only probes deeply enough.

A PAWN END GAME

We are inclined to undervalue Pawn endings. They contain fewer possibilities: we know the various little *tempo* tricks, we are familiar with the rules of the "protected passed Pawn" and the "outside passed Pawn"—what is there left? Only the exact counting to see who queens first?

Just the same, it is precisely in the Pawn endings that radical errors of judgment are often committed—all the more serious as the difference between winning and losing may be a single *tempo*.

The present position is from a game between G. Van Keulen and G. R. D. Van Doesburgh, Laren, Holland.

White is a Pawn down, but his King takes up a mighty position and can unimpeded capture Black's King Knight Pawn and so establish a passed Pawn. One is consequently inclined to judge White's chances as the better.

Our investigation will reveal otherwise. The chances for

either side turn on small things. If White were allowed two moves, P-QN4 and P-KN4, he'd not only be beyond danger of losing but also able with good chances to play for a win. Two Black moves, however, ... P-QR4 and ... P-KR5, are sufficient to secure the win for Black.

Thus we have already given away the critical moves. Their significance is easily explained:

(1) ... P-KR5 holds down White's King side;

(2) P-KN4 forestalls this intention;

(3) P-QN4 delays the emergence of a Black passed Pawn as, for ... P-B4 and ... P-Q5, preparation by ... P-N3 is then required;

(4) ... P-QR4 hampers this last plan.

Note, too, that *zugzwang* can arise only for White's King! Black's shuttles at will between QB1 and Q1 as White's K-K7 is worth no more than K-K6 which will always be possible.

Now we shall take up successively the different systems, beginning with the simplest and most obvious.

A. The Primitive Method

1 K-K6, an immediate "pass" at the Black King Knight Pawn, is met by *1* ... K-B2; *2* K-B6, P-B4! Already White cannot make the capture as Black's Queen Pawn simply goes through. On *3* K-K5, K-B3, moreover, Black's extra Pawn insures a clear win.

B. First Compromise

1 P-QN4   P-R5

Both sides have made one of the "desirable" moves. Having delayed the emergence of the hostile passed Pawn, White may retry the primitive method.

2 K-K6   K-B2

Note that 2 ... P-N3 is not yet possible; 3 K-Q6 wins the key Bishop Pawn.

3 K-B6   P-N3

4 KxP   ....

Here White has regained his Pawn and will get the King Rook Pawn. It seems he is on the way to win. Black contrives, however, just in time to guard the latter indirectly—and, by that, he wins.

4	P-B4	7 PxP	PxP
5 PxP	PxP	8 K-B4	K-Q3
6 K-N5	P-Q5	9 K-K4	K-B4
		10 K-Q3	K-Q4

In the outcome White's King will be forced into a stalemate position on Q1, he must eventually move his King Knight Pawn, and mate in three follows, with ... P-N8(Q) mate.

From the last diagram, if White sets out for Black's King Rook Pawn, counting on returning just in time, he is met by a well-known but treacherous twist: 4 K-N5, P-B4; 5 PxP, PxP; 6 KxRP, P-Q5; 7 PxP, P-B5! and Black's Pawn goes through.

C. A Sharp Continuation

(Resume from first diagram)

1 P-QN4   P-R5   *2* P-N5   . . . .

This sharp move threatens completely to upset Black's win-ning methods as seen in the previous variations.

2 . . . .   PxP   *3* KxP   . . . .

Now things look much better for White as Black's doubled Pawn is not worth much and White's King continues to have attacking chances on both wings.

3 . . . .   K-K2!

Black rightly disregards the vulnerability of his Queen Knight Pawn. Getting a passed Pawn, he wins the race: e.g., *4* K-B5, K-K3! *5* KxP, K-K4; *6* K-B5, K-B5; *7* K-Q6, K-N6; *8* K-B7, KxP; *9* KxP, KxP; *10* P-B4, K-N6; *11* P-B5, P-R6; *12* P-B6, P-R7; *13* P-B7, P-Q8(Q) *with check.*

4 K-K5   . . . .

White's only move: he cannot permit Black's King to pass.

4 . . . .   P-R4!

Not solely a "waiting" move.

Now the play can follow 5 courses.

1) 5 K-Q5, K-B3; *6* K-B5, P-N5! 7 PxP, PxP; *8* KxP, K-B4; *9* K-N5, K-B5; *10* K-N6, K-N6; *11* KxP, KxP; *12* P-R4, KxP; *13* P-R5, K-N6; *14* P-R6, P-R6; *15* P-R7, P-R7; *16* P-R8(Q), P-Q8(Q) and again *with check*. Black has just made it.

2) 5 K-Q5, K-B3; *6* P-R3 (preventing the preceding, but the *tempo* gained is lost on the move itself), K-B4; 7 K-B5, K-B5; *8* KxP, K-N6; *9* K-N6, KxP; *10* KxNP, KxP; *11* P-B4, K-N6; *12* P-B5, P-R6; *13* P-B6, P-R7; *14* P-B7, P-Q8(Q) again with check!

3) 5 P-R3, P-N3; *6* K-Q5, K-Q2 (now White's King cannot keep its ground); 7 K-K5, K-B3; *8* K-B6 (8 K-Q4, K-Q3 and Black must get in ... K-B4 and ... P-N5 to decide the issue), K-B4; *9* KxP, K-B5; *10* K-N5, KxP; *11* KxP, P-N5 and Black will win.

4) 5 K-B4, K-B3; *6* K-N4, P-N4; 7 K-B3 (on 7 K-R5, K-B4; *8* K-R6, Black wins by 8 ... P-KN5), K-B4; *8* K-K3, P-KN5; *9* PxPch, KxP; *10* K-B2, K-B5; *11* K-K2, K-K5; *12* K-Q2, K-Q4; *13* K-Q3, P-N3; *14* P-R3, K-B4 and Black can break through.

5) 5 K-K4, K-K3 leads into the variations already discussed.

D. White's Best

(Resume from first diagram)

We have seen that White's P-QN4-5 sets Black knotty problems. Now we try this push only after proper preparation. Black's task becomes even more difficult; and, though the chances remain on his side, White succeeds, by problem moves, in bringing about a draw.

1 P-QN4   P-R5   *2* P-R4   ....

This way P-N5 gains in force. White regains his Pawn without more ado.

         2 ....   K-B1

Or 2 ... P-R3; 3 P-R5, paralyzing the Black Pawn majority whereafter White's King can proceed King sideward safely.

3 P-N5	PxP	4 PxP	K-Q1
		5 KxP	....

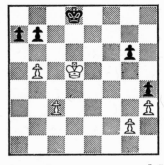

Materially, the game is now even, and White's King still stands more favorably. Yet White's chances are not correspondingly better. His chances at the King side are forfeited: as soon as his King moves far enough from the center, ... P-QR4 gives Black the outside passed Pawn.

5 ... P-R4 too soon loses: 6 PxP e.p., PxP; 7 K-B6! And, too late: e.g., 5 ... K-Q2; 6 K-B5, K-B2; 7 P-B4, P-R4, success is far from assured: 8 PxP e.p., PxP; 9 K-Q5! P-R4; 10 K-B5, and White wins the Rook Pawn—or 9 ... K-N3; 10 K-Q6, and White promotes his passed Pawn.

Therefore Black dare play ... P-R4 only when White's Bishop Pawn has advanced to B5 or Black's King is on that square. Hence, Black aims for ... K-QN3.

5	K-Q2	7 P-B4	P-N4
6 K-B5	K-B2	8 K-Q5!	....

8 K-N4, K-N3 grants Black his objective of either 9 P-B5ch or 10 ... K-QB4, as in the last note.

| 8 .... | K-N3 | 9 K-Q6 | K-R4 |

After 9 ... P-R3; 10 PxP, KxP (forced); 11 K-B7! K-R4 (11 ... P-N3; 12 K-B6, K-R4; 13 K-Q5 and 14 P-B5); 12 KxP,

K-N5; *13* K-B6, KxP; *14* K-Q6, White easily arrives in time:
14 ... K-Q5; *15* K-K6, K-K5; *16* K-B6, K-B5; *17* K-N6, P-N5
Drawn.

10 K-B5   ....

10 K-B7 is a loss for White: *10* ... K-N5; *11* KxP, KxP; *12*
KxP, KxP, and Black arrives one *tempo* earlier.

10 ....   K-R5

10 ... P-N3ch is also possible with about the same consequences as shall soon appear.

11 K-Q4!   ....

11 K-Q5 loses: *11* ... K-N5; *12* K-Q4, P-N3! and either *13*
K-Q5, K-B6; *14* P-B5, PxP; *15* KxP, K-N6; *16* K-B6, K-B5;
17 P-N6, PxP; *18* KxP, K-Q6—or *13* K-Q3, K-N6; *14* K-Q4,
K-B7! *15* P-B5, PxPch; *16* KxP, K-N6; *17* K-B6, K-B5 as Black
wins the race for the King-side.

11 ....   P-N3

After *11* ... K-N6; *12* P-B5, White's Bishop Pawn marches
on; and, after *11* ... K-N5; *12* K-Q5, P-N3; *13* K-Q4, Black
makes no further headway as White retains the opposition.

After the text move the situation appears critical for White. On *12* K-Q5 or K-Q3, K-N6 or *12* K-B3, K-R6, White is in trouble.

12 K-K4!!   . . . .

By assuming the distant opposition, White forces a draw: *12* . . . K-N5; *13* K-Q4 or *12* . . . K-N6; *13* K-Q3 or *12* . . . K-R6; *13* K-K3 or, in this latter case, *13* K-B5.

If we now, incidentally, have another look at the diagram after *10* K-B5, we see that *10* . . . P-N3ch likewise produces a draw after *11* K-Q5, K-R5; *12* K-K4!

This Variation D, consequently, leads to a draw and, in fact, in a surprising manner. In viewing the first position, who would ever have given a thought to a possible distant opposition!

Still our investigation has not covered all. About every Pawn end game, of which the outcome has not been determined beforehand, volumes could be written. In order not to stretch out too much, we present the rest in condensed form.

(Resume from first diagram)

E. *1* P-QN4, P-R5; *2* P-R4, K-B1; *3* P-R5 is sharper, to be sure, but not so strong as D: *3* . . . K-Q1; *4* P-R6, K-B1! *5* PxPch, KxP (e.g., *6* K-K6, K-B2; *7* K-B6, P-B4! *8* PxP, P-R4).

F. *1* P-KN4, PxP; *2* PxP, P-R4! (White would win if permitted *3* P-N4—analogous to Variation D); *3* P-N5, K-B1; *4* K-K6, K-B2 (*4* . . . P-N3; *5* K-Q6, K-N2; *6* P-R4 is in White's favor); *5* K-B6, P-B4; *6* KxP, P-Q5; *7* PxP, PxP, and Black has only

slight winning chances: e.g., 8 K-B5, P-Q6; 9 P-N6, P-Q7; *10*
P-N7, P-Q8(Q); *11* P-N8(Q).

G. *1* P-KN4, PxP; *2* PxP, P-R4! *3* P-N5, K-B1; *4* P-N3 (to
enforce P-N4 anyway: *4* P-R3 fails against *4 ...* P-R5), K-N1!
5 P-R3, K-R2; *6* P-N4, PxP; *7* RPxP, K-N3; *8* K-K6, K-N4, and
again Black has only small winning chances: e.g., *9* K-B6, K-B5;
10 KxP, KxP; *11* K-B5, P-Q5; *12* P-N6, P-Q6; *13* P-N7, P-Q7;
14 P-N8(Q), P-Q8(Q); *15* Q-N7ch.

Our conclusion, therefore, reads first, that White achieves a
draw by a narrow margin, by means of *1* P-QN4, followed by
2 P-QR4 and *3* P-N5.

And, second, that we're dealing here with a difficult Pawn
end game in which one can very easily make mistakes.

A TRIO OF SNAPSHOTS

Herewith are three positions from the Clare Benedict Tournament. Each represents a different type of end game. The
first is one of pure technique. The second is technical with a
combinational angle. And the last is a purely combinational
one. But all of them feature unexpected turns and a surprise
point.

QUEEN'S GAMBIT DECLINED

	H. JOHNER			R. G. WADE	
	White			*Black*	
1	P-Q4	P-Q4	*11*	BxP	N-N5
2	P-QB4	P-K3	*12*	Q-N3	QN-B3
3	N-QB3	N-KB3	*13*	B-K2	NxB
4	B-N5	P-B4	*14*	QxN	Q-N5ch
5	N-B3	PxQP	*15*	Q-Q2	B-B4
6	KNxP	P-K4	*16*	QxQ	NxQ
7	N-B3	P-Q5	*17*	O-O	P-B3
8	N-Q5	B-K2	*18*	P-QR3	B-Q6
9	NxB	QxN	*19*	KR-K1	BxB
10	P-K3	PxP	*20*	RxB	N-Q6

21	N-Q4	N-B5	56	P-R6	R-Q2
22	R-K3	O-O-O	57	R-N2	R-K2
23	N-N5	R-Q7	58	KxP	R-K8
24	P-QN4	P-QR3	59	R-QB2	R-Q8ch
25	N-B3	KR-Q1	60	K-B3	R-KN8
26	P-B5	R/1-Q5	61	R-K2	K-B4
27	K-B1	N-Q4	62	R-K5ch	K-Q3
28	NxN	RxN	63	RxNP	RxPch
29	K-K1	K-B2	64	K-Q4	R-KR6
30	R-K2	R/7-Q6	65	R-R5	K-B3
31	R-B2	K-B3	66	R-R7	RxP
32	P-QR4	R-QN6	67	K-K5	R-R5
33	R-B4	R-Q5	68	R-KN7	K-B4
34	RxR	PxR	69	R-B7ch	K-N5
35	P-N5ch	PxP	70	K-B6	RxP
36	PxPch	RxP	71	RxP	R-N5
37	R-R8	RxP	72	R-QB7	P-B5
38	K-Q2	R-Q4	73	K-K5	P-N4
39	R-B8ch	K-N3	74	K-K4	R-N6
40	K-Q3	R-Q2	75	R-B8	K-N6
41	R-B1	K-R2	76	R-B5	K-N7
42	R-R1ch	K-N1	77	R-B8	P-B6
43	R-QN1	R-Q3	78	K-K3	P-N5
44	R-K1	K-B2	79	K-K-B2	R-N7ch
45	R-B1ch	K-Q2	80	K-B1	R-QB7
46	R-QN1	P-QN3	81	R-KN8	R-B5
47	P-B4	K-B2	82	K-B2	K-B7
48	R-B1ch	K-N2	83	R-Q8	R-K5
49	R-K1	R-Q2	84	R-B8ch	K-Q6
50	R-QN1	P-B4	85	R-Q8ch	R-Q5
51	P-N3	P-N3	86	R-KN8	R-R5
52	R-N2	R-Q4	87	R-Q8ch	K-K5
53	R-N1	P-QN4	88	R-K8ch	K-B4
54	P-R4	K-N3	89	R-B8ch	K-K5
55	P-R5	R-Q3			

About the last 60 moves of this end game all sorts of observations could be made, of course; but we confine ourselves to the final phase.

Black has two connected passed Pawns. At first glance, therefore, a simple job; but, when looking more closely, one keeps encountering difficulties and is even inclined to conclude that Black cannot win. For that matter, a number of analogous positions do end in a draw. The truth lies in the middle: Black wins, but by a highly problematic method: in order to win on the King side, Black's King moves to the Queen side.

Even so, the whole process works in a strictly logical manner. The main point of the solution lies concealed in this, that Black wins when his Rook arrives on the seventh rank with check while his King stands no further removed from the board's edge than Black's QB8.

Consequently, let us consider the second position.

1 ....   R-B7ch

Now there are three possibilities. The least favorable is
2 K-N3? (or the analogous 2 K-K3?) after which there follows
simply 2 ... R-N7ch; 3 K-R4, P-B7; 4 R-KB8, P-N6 and 5 ...
R-N8.

Variant 1

2 K-B1   ....

We shall take up 2 K-N1 presently.

2 ....   R-KN7

Now White's Rook can stand watch on the King Knight file
or check or cut off Black's King.

Sub-variant A

3 R-N7   P-N6   4 R-B7ch   ....

4 R-KB7, R-B7ch; 5 K-N1 (not 5 K-K1? R-K7ch; 6 K-B1,
P-N7ch), K-Q8 comes to practically the same thing.

4 ....   K-Q8   5 R-KN7   ....

After 5 R-Q7ch, R-Q7, it is even easier: 6 R-KN7, P-N7ch;
7 K-N1, K-K8, etc., or 6 R-KB7, R-B7ch; 7 K-N1, K-K8, etc.
And the same holds for 5 R-KB7, R-B7ch; 6 K-N1, K-K8.

5 ....   R-B7ch   6 K-N1   K-K8

It cannot be done without sacrificing a Pawn.

7 RxP   R-B8ch   8 K-R2   ....

8 ....   K-B7

Not 8 ... P-B7? *9* R-K3ch, K-Q7; *10* K-N2! But now Black wins with *9* R-N8, R-K8; *10* R-QR8, K-B8, etc., or *10* R-KB8, K-K7, etc.

Sub-variant B

3 R-B8ch   K-Q7

4 R-K8   ....

Under no circumstances must White pursue Black's King further as it escapes to KN6: e.g., *4* R-Q8ch, K-K6; *5* R-KN8, R-QR7 (with threat of mate); *6* R-K8ch, K-B5 (and threat now of 7 ... R-R8ch; *8* K-B2, P-N6 mate); *7* R-B8ch, K-N6. And *4* R-KN8, K-K6 comes to the same thing.

| *4* .... | P-N6 | *5* R-Q8ch | ..... |

Now there is not so much harm in the checks as Black's King no longer has a place to hide. But White is compelled to give check, anyway: e.g., *5* R-K8, R-K7; *6* R-Q8ch, K-B6; *7* R-B8ch, K-N5 and Black's Rook can now handle the situation single-handed: *8* R-KN8, P-N7ch; *9* K-N1, R-K8ch; *10* K-B2, R-B8ch, etc.

| *5* .... | K-B8 |

And here we are at a position in the winning Sub-variant A.

Sub-variant C

| *3* R-Q8 | P-N6 |

This continuation also leads at once to the winning Sub-variant A.

Variant II

| (*1* .... | R-B7ch) | *2* K-N1 | R-N7ch |

Now it appears by *3* K-B1, P-N6, we can lead automatically into Variant I; but White can play differently.

3 K-R1!   ....

The point is that White's King is now "stalemated" so that Black cannot have his King march to KB5 because of the well-known "cling check"—e.g., *3 ... K-Q8; 4* R-Q8ch, K-K8; *5* R-Q1ch! K-B7; *6* R-B1ch! K-N6; *7* RxPch! etc.

3 ....   P-N6

With the threat of *4 ...* R-R7ch; *5* K-N1, P-B7ch, etc.

4 R-B8ch R-B7   *5* R-KR8 ....

Otherwise, *5 ...* R-R7ch decides.

5 ....   K-N7

And now Black wins as again his Rook can handle the queening alone. On checks, Black's King comes back down the Rook and Knight files.

With the experience now gained we can probably manage Position No. 1. There followed from that position this play in the actual game.

90 R-K8ch K-Q6

91 R-Q8ch ....

It is clear that White cannot play a "waiting game"—*91* R-K7? R-R7ch, etc. But why doesn't he play here *91* K-N3? The answer is *91 ...* R-R7! (threatening *92 ...* R-N7ch); *92* KxP (checks merely drive Black's King to KB8, the main objection to *91* K-N3), P-B7; *93* R-KB8, K-K7; *94* R-K8ch,

K-Q8 (also 94 ... K-B8 is good); 95 R-KB8, K-K8; 96 R-K8ch, R-K7, and Black wins.

| 91 .... | R-Q5 | 92 R-QR8 | .... |

White's Rook could also "bide" on the King Knight file.

| 92 .... | R-QB5 |

With the threat of 93 ... R-B7ch, which wins.

93 R-Q8ch   ....

Not 93 R-R6ch because of 93 ... R-B6 and 94 R-B7ch next. Nor 93 K-N3 because of 93 ... R-B7!

| 93 .... | K-B7 | 94 K-N3 | .... |

Or 94 R-Q7, K-B8 after which 95 K·N3 becomes compulsory, anyway, because of the threat of 95 ... R-B7ch.

94 ....   K-B8!

Note the resemblance to our second diagram.

Perhaps the question may be asked if all this could not just as well have been brought off on the Queen file. The answer is "No." For in that case White's Rook would have been able to defend from the flank, operating from QR1 and QR2 (which requires the White King to be posted at KB2).

95 R-Q7 . . . .

Two other possibilities call for our attention here.

1) 95 R-KB8, so as to make it a draw on 95 ... R-B7? with 96 KxP, P-B7; 97 K-N3, etc. Black continues, however, with 95 ... K-Q8! 96 R-Q8ch, K-K8; 97 R-K8ch, K-B8; 98 R-QR8, R-B8; 99 KxP, P-B7; 100 K-N3, K-N8, etc. Or 99 R-KR2, K-N8 and 100 ... P-B7! Nor in this variation is a "waiting line" possible: 95 R-KB8, K-Q8! 96 R-B7, R-B7; 97 KxP, P-B7; 98 K-N3, K-K8 or, likewise, 96 R-QR8, R-B7; 97 R-R1ch, K-K7.

2) 95 R-QR8, K-Q8 (95 ... R-B7? leads to a draw after 96 KxP, P-B7; 97 K-N3, K-Q8; 98 R-R1ch, K-K7; 99 K-N2); 96 R-R1ch, R-B8; 97 R-R4, K-K7, and again it just works (98 R-R2ch, K-B8 or 98 KxP, P-B7).

95 . . . . R-B7!

The key to the solution.

96 KxP	P-B7	98 K-N3	K-K8
97 R-KB7	K-Q8	99 R-K7ch	R-K7
		100 R-QR7	. . . .

The last point now comes up.

100 . . . . R-K6ch Resigns

Because Black now queens, but at least White did reach the 100th move.

RUY LOPEZ

	C. B. VAN DEN BERG				W. NIEPHAUS	
	White				*Black*	
1	P-K4	P-K4		13	N-B1	BPxP
2	N-KB3	N-QB3		14	PxP	QR-B1
3	B-N5	P-QR3		15	B-N1	P-Q4
4	B-R4	N-B3		16	KPxP	P-K5
5	O-O	B-K2		17	N-N5	BxP
6	R-K1	P-QN4		18	NxP	NxN
7	B-N3	P-Q3		19	BxN	BxB
8	P-B3	O-O		20	RxB	B-B3
9	P-KR3	QN-R4		21	N-N3	KR-K1
10	B-B2	P-B4		22	B-B4	Q-Q2
11	P-Q4	Q-B2		23	B-K5	BxB
12	QN-Q2	B-N2		24	PxB	QxQch
				25	RxQ	....

White has a Pawn plus. He cannot, however, protect his
Queen-side Pawns by direct methods. Hence he resorts to
indirect, combinative methods.

25 ....   R-B7

Not 25 ... N-B5; 26 P-N3, NxP; 27 QR-K1, P-B3; 28 P-B4,
and White wins.

26 R-Q6   R-R1?

It is due to this last move that White is enabled to reap the fruits of his tactics. Black's only chance of salvation consists in 26 ... RxNP; 27 RxP, RxRP; 28 R-QN4, R-R8ch; 29 K-R2, N-N6; 30 RxR, NxR; 31 RxP, N-B7. Then, with the remaining Pawns all on one side of the board, Black has excellent drawing chances, though a similar end game, Taimanov—Stahlberg, Challengers Tournament, 1953, was won by White.

27 P-K6!   PxP

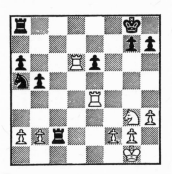

28 R/4xP   . . . .

White bases his counter-action principally on the seventh rank. Thus, 28 ... RxNP is refuted by 29 R-Q7, RxRP (29 ... R-KB1; 30 N-K4 as in the game); 30 R/6-K7; e.g., 30 ... N-B5; 31 RxPch, K-B1; 32 R/Q-B7ch, K-K1; 33 R-N7, K-B1; 34 RxRP, K-N1; 35 R/N-N7ch, K-B1; 36 N-R5, and 37 R-R8 mate.

28 . . . .   R-KB1   29 N-K4   . . . .

Naturally, White does not permit his opponent to crash in on his KB2.

29 . . . .   N-N2

Here, too, 29 ... RxNP is pernicious: 30 R-Q7, R-B2 (does not help); 31 R-K8ch, R-B1; 32 R/8-K7, etc.

30 RxP   ....

Simpler is *30* R-Q7 as *30* ... N-B4 gives no relief: *31* NxN, R/1xP? *32* R-K8ch, etc. Contrast the game continuation.

30 ....   N-B4!

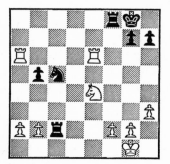

A particularly pretty riposte, which brings to mind the proverb: "Dig a pit, and get caught in it yourself." After *31* NxN? R/1xP, it is White who faces the miseries of the "seventh rank" and so has to resort to draw by perpetual check.

31 R/R-B6!

The saving move.[1]

31	R-B8ch	*32* K-R2	NxR
		33 RxR	....

White won easily with his material plus.

[1] We beg to differ. Surmounting the fear of a near-perpetual is *31* NxN, R/1xP *32* R-R8ch, K-B2 *33* R-R7ch, K-B1 (or .... K-N1 *34* R-K8ch, R-B1 *35* RxRch, etc.) *34* R-Q6! and White wins.—I.A.H.

BENONI COUNTER-GAMBIT DEFERRED

	J. H. DONNER			H. JOHNER	
	White			*Black*	
1	P-Q4	N-KB3	21	B-R3	PxP
2	P-QB4	P-B4	22	BxQ	PxQ
3	P-Q5	P-Q3	23	B-B6	R-R4
4	N-QB3	P-KN3	24	RxQP	P-B5
5	P-KN3	B-N2	25	R-Q1	BxN
6	B-N2	O-O	26	PxB	N/2xP
7	N-B3	P-QR3	27	B-R3	R-KB4
8	P-QR4	Q-B2	28	BxQP	NxP
9	O-O	P-K4	29	R-K1	N/6-Q4
10	PxP e.p.	BxP	30	R-K8ch	K-B2
11	N-Q5	BxN	31	R-K4	R-B3
12	PxB	QN-Q2	32	B-K8ch	K-N1
13	P-R5	P-QN4	33	B-R3	R-R1
14	PxP e.p.	QNxP	34	B-N5	R-QB1
15	N-Q2	P-QR4	35	R-QB1	P-B6
16	N-N1	Q-Q2	36	BxP	NxB
17	N-B3	P-R5	37	RxN/4	P-B7
18	P-K4	N-K1	38	R-R7	R-N3
19	Q-Q3	N-B2	39	K-B1	R-N8
20	R-Q1	P-B4	40	K-K2	N-B6ch

After heavy time pressure, the players reached this position. It is, therefore, not exactly of great importance to remark that

Black could have won quickly by *40* ... N-N5 (*41* K-Q2, R-Q1ch and *42* ... R/1-Q8). In a certain sense, it is fortunate that Black overlooked this continuation as we would otherwise have been deprived of witnessing the combinational phase of the game which follows.

41 K-Q2 ....

41 K-Q3 loses to *41* ... N-N4; *42* R-R5, R-B6ch, and *43* ... RxB.

41 .... N-K5ch

Here *41* ... N-N4; *42* R-R5 produces nothing. Following the text move, however, the struggle grows particularly complicated because White's King can move three different ways:

1) *42* K-K3, see the game;

2) *42* K-K2, R-B6! and White has no parry to the threat of *43* ... RxB: e.g., *43* P-B3, RxB; *44* R/7xR, RxR; *45* PxN, R-KR8 —or *43* R-R8ch, K-B2; *44* R-R7ch, K-B3; *45* B-K7ch, K-K3, etc.

3) *42* K-Q3, NxPch; *43* K-K3, R-B6ch; *44* KxN, RxB; *45* R/7xR, RxR; *46* R-QB3, R-KR8!—or *43* K-K2, R-B6; *44* R-R8ch (*44* B-N2, RxB; *45* KxN, R-QN8; *46* R-QR1, RxR/R8!), K-N2; *45* R-R7ch, K-B3; *46* R-R6ch, K-K4; *47* R-R5ch, K-K3; *48* R-R6ch, K-Q2; *49* R-Q6ch, K-B2; *50* KxN, RxB, etc.—or *43* K-Q2, N-K5ch; *44* K-Q3, N-Q3; *45* RxBP, R-N6ch; *46* K-Q2, N-B5ch; *47* K-K2 (*47* K-B1 loses to *47* ... R-KB6), RxB! *48* RxR, R-K1ch and *49* ... NxR.

42 K-K3 N-Q3

Now Black threatens *43* ... N-B5ch as well as *43* ... N-N4, and the finish is forced.

43 RxBP	RxR	*45* KxK4	R-K7ch
44 BxN	R-N6ch	*46* K-Q4	RxBP
		47 P-R4	R-Q7ch

With the full Exchange ahead, this end game is now won for Black. Unfortunately the Nestor of the Swiss team (and

of the Benedict Tournament as a whole) blundered after
48 K-B4, R-K6; *49* R-R8ch, K-B2; *50* R-R7ch with *50* ... K-K3?
(instead of *50* ... K-K1) and, after *51* R-K7ch, had to content
himself with a draw.

THE EXCHANGE—PLUS AND MINUS

A fine study in the use of the advantage of the Exchange
under very adverse factors: a Pawn minus and also a deficit in
most of the positional considerations.

In Dr. Euwe's theories of chess play, the value of the Exchange is somewhat less highly regarded than in the past, even
the recent past. In the middle game, indeed, he has suggested
that a minor piece may give battle to a Rook on equal or very
nearly equal terms. So this exposition of the winning power
of the Exchange is highly significant, the more so that the
lesser side has so many other factors in its favor. The summary
of the positional factors is in itself a worth-while lesson. And
the whole, with a generous coverage of both tactical and strategical features, is a valuable demonstration of what is vaguely
called "technique"—and what may here be termed "the higher
technique."

In all this both players, as well as the commentator, exhibit
some remarkably impressive chess.

Yugoslav Championship

December, 1953

KING'S INDIAN DEFENSE

by transposition

VASYA PIRC		SVETOZAR GLIGORICH	
White		*Black*	
1 N-KB3	N-KB3	*5* O-O	PxP
2 P-KN3	P-Q3	*6* NxP	P-KN3
3 P-Q4	QN-Q2	*7* P-N3	B-N2
4 B-N2	P-K4	*8* B-N2	O-O

9	N-QB3	R-K1		
10	P-K4	N-B4		
11	R-K1	P-B3		
12	Q-Q2	Q-N3		
13	P-KR3	B-Q2		
14	QR-Q1	QR-Q1		
15	K-R2	QB-B1		
16	P-B3	Q-B2		
17	Q-B2	Q-N3		
18	N/4-K2	N/4-Q2		
19	QxQ	NxQ		
20	P-B4	P-Q4		
21	P-K5	N/3-Q2		
22	N-Q4	N-B1		
23	P-QR4	P-QR4		
24	N/3-K2	B-Q2		
25	N-B1	N-K3		

26	N-Q3	N-R1		
27	NxN	PxN		
28	P-B4	PxP		
29	PxP	N-N3		
30	N-B5	B-QB1		
31	B-KB1	B-B1		
32	N-K4	NxRP		
33	N-B6ch	K-B2		
34	NxR	RxN		
35	B-R1	B-N5		
36	R-K3	K-K2		
37	P-R4	B-Q2		
38	P-R5	R-QR1		
39	PxP	PxP		
40	P-N4	R-R1ch		
41	R-R3	RxRch		
42	KxR	N-B4		

White has the Exchange for a Pawn. From the purely materialistic point of view, White therefore stands better. For the Exchange equals 1½ Pawns. That is, according to the old-fashioned way of assessing positions of this type. Only in special cases, must it be added, do positional factors compensate for a plus in material.

Yet nowadays opinions differ in regard to the Exchange, in this sense, that the emphasis is placed less on the factor of material than on that of position. As positional factors in the contest between Rook and minor piece there are considered, among others: (1) the presence of passed Pawns; (2) the presence of other minor pieces; (3) the presence of strongholds (or outposts); (4) the Pawn configuration; and (5) the position of the King.

(1) The passed Pawns are important to the side with the minor piece especially because these can occupy the attention of the Rook to such extent as to eliminate the differential in values between the Rook and the minor piece.

(2) The presence of other minor pieces also has a neutralizing tendency. Conversely, in the contest between Rook and a single minor piece, the superiority of the Rook is so paramount that it cannot be offset sometimes even by two Pawns.

(3) The presence of strongholds is indispensable to a proper development of the power of the minor piece. For a Knight that can be continually driven off by the Rook does not come into its own.

(4) The Pawn configuration may give the Rook occasion for going off on a foray. Pawns difficult to protect signify a serious handicap to the side with the minor piece.

(5) The position of the King is likewise especially important to the weaker side. For the Rook, particularly in combination with other pieces (including a King), is a dangerous offensive weapon.

Examining the current position on the score of these positional factors, we must come to the conclusion that the majority of the factors are in Black's favor. He has a passed Pawn and threatens even to acquire still another. There are minor pieces on the board. And Black possesses strongholds for his minor pieces (QN5 and QB4 among others). In contrast, however, the position of Black's King is definitely insecure: shut in on the first and second ranks. Therefore, if White is to win, it is this factor which must decide. In fact, we shall observe the attack motif weaving throughout this entire end game.

43 B-Q4   ....

White's first step emphasizes the attack motif, for which he conveys his Bishop to the other wing.

His move, moreover, prevents the advance of Black's Rook Pawn. Consider: 43 ... P-R5? 44 R-R1 and

(1) 44 ... P-QN4; 45 PxP, PxP; 46 R-N1, N-R3; 47 RxB! etc.
(2) 44 ... P-R6; 45 R-N1, N-R3; 46 RxB!

43 ....   N-N6   44 B-B2   ....

Here White's Bishop stands very well for attacking purposes. 45 B-R4ch, K-K1; 46 B-Q3 is threatened, winning a Pawn. Consequently, Black still has no time for advancing his passed Pawn.

44 ....   N-B4

Black protects his Queen Bishop and also observes White's Q3.

45 R-N1   ....

Again White prevents ... P-R5 and also threatens RxB!

45 ....   N-K5   46 B-R4ch   K-B2

46 ... P-KN4 leads to a quick loss after 47 B-Q3! by which White gains a Pawn and establishes the needed passed Pawn.

47 B-Q3   N-B6

Black must remain active. After 47 ... N-B4; 48 B-QB2, he would be halted on the Queen side, whereupon White would gain a free hand on the other wing.

White's strategy now could be to set up a mating attack by R-KR1, B-B6 and K-N3, except that Black, thanks to his last moves, holds just sufficient counter-measures in reserve. Note: 48 R-KR1, P-B4! 49 B-B6, B-B3! 50 R-R2, N-K5, and White gets no further.

In the original position given, if White's King stood on KN3, instead of KR3, this variation would have brought about a speedy decision.

48 R-QR1   P-B4

Black aims to follow up with ... B-B3 and thus guard against a later execution of the attack just mentioned. A drawback of his last move, however, is that now the possibility of establishing connected passed Pawns is out of the picture.

49 B-K1   ....

For the time being White limits himself to the defense. He must first bring his King to the other wing, to lessen somewhat the power of Black's passed Rook Pawn.

49 ....   B-B3   *50* K-N3   ....

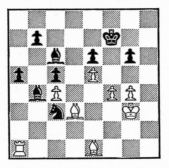

It is instructive to investigate what effect the exchange of one or more of the minor pieces might have at this juncture.

Thus Black might try: *50* ... B-K5; *51* BxB, NxBch; *52* K-B3, but he stands to lose after *52* ... N-B6; *53* K-K3 because of the threat of losing a piece on *54* K-Q3. (*53* ... P-QN4 is no help in view of *54* BxN, BxB; *55* PxP!) And, on *52* ... N-Q7ch, White wins a Pawn by *53* BxN, BxB; *54* R-Q1 and *55* R-Q7ch. Or, finally, *52* ... BxB only loses a Pawn by either *53* KxN, B-N5; *54* R-R1, K-N2; *55* R-Q1—or *53* ... B-B6; *54* R-R1, K-N2; *55* R-Q1, B-Q5; *56* R-QN1.

And on *50* ... N-K5ch White can seize the occasion to exchange; for, after *51* BxN, BxKB; *52* BxB, RPxB; *53* R-R5, he stands to accumulate Pawns by *53* ... P-N6; *54* R-N5, B-B7; *55* RxPch or *53* ... P-N3; *54* R-N5, B-Q6; *55* RxP/6, BxP; *56* R-B6 (also very strong is *56* R-N7ch, K-K1; *57* K-R4, followed by the advance of White's King), P-N6; *57* RxBP (for, on *57* ... P-N7, White has *58* R-B7ch and *59* R-QN7).

A number of these variations wind up in an end game of Rook versus Bishop, with Pawns equal. Such present no special technical problem for White, for he can always, by bringing his King in closer, effect an exchange of Rook for Bishop and Pawn and then win the resulting end game.

As a side issue, it should be noted that 50 ... P-R5 costs a Pawn: 51 K-B2, P-R6 (or this advance may be forced by 52 B-B2); 52 BxN, BxB; 53 RxP.

50 ....   N-R5   51 K-B2   ....

White does not exchange Bishops as that results only in advancing and strengthening the passed Pawn.

51 ....   N-N7

Black stays on the offensive. He must; for, after 51 ... N-N3, White continues the same way as in the game (K-K3 and B-Q2) and Black cannot make a single counter-blow count because of the inactive position of his Knight.

52 K-K3   ....

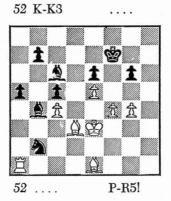

52 ....   P-R5!

Forward at last! And, indeed, what else? Exchanging Knight for Bishop here gains nothing at all. For, after 52 ... NxB; 53 KxN, White actually threatens 54 BxB, RPxB; 55 R-R5, and there is no adequate reply: e.g., 53 ... BxB; 54 RxB, P-R5; 55 K-B3, B-B6; 56 P-N5, B-B3; 57 R-K2, B-B6; 58 R-QR2, B-B3; 59 R-R2, K-N2; 60 R-Q2, K-B2; 61 R-Q8, K-N2; 62 R-QR8, K-B2; 63 R-R5, and White wins a Pawn.

Or, on *61* ... K-K2, Black lands in *zugzwang* after *62* R-KR8, K-B2; *63* R-R7ch, K-B1 (*63* ... K-N1; *64* R-K7); *64* K-N2.

Or if Black tries *53* ... P-R5 (instead of *53* ... BxB), he can be maneuvered out of position by *54* B-Q2, K-K2 (not *54* ... P-R6? *55* B-B1); *55* R-QN1, B-R6; *56* B-R5, K-B2; *57* K-B3 and *58* R-QR1.

53 B-Q2!   ....

To bring the Bishop to QB1.

| *53* .... | P-R6 | *54* B-QB1 | N-Q8ch |

A new resource again for Black.

55 K-K2   N-N7

After *55* ... N-B6ch, Black's Rook Pawn soon goes: *56* K-B1, P-R7; *57* B-N2.

56 P-N5   ....

White aims to reserve a *tempo* in case Black should ever try ... B-KB6 later. It is remarkable that the text move detracts nothing from White's King-side Pawn majority. That is a fact since the move, P-KB5, will, under proper conditions, create a passed Pawn.

56 ....   K-N2

Not best. Properly *56* ... NxB; *57* KxN, P-N4 transposes back into the actual game.

57 R-R2   ....

But White returns the favor. He can win more quickly with *57* BxN, PxB; *58* R-R8, P-N4 (else *59* R-QB8); *59* R-R7ch,

K-N1; *60* BxP by virtue of his own passed Pawn. Apparently, fault begets fault!

57 .... NxB

On *57* ... N-R5 there follows *58* K-B1, N-B6; *59* R-R1, after which Black must lose his Rook Pawn.

58 KxN P-N4!

Passed Pawns!

59 BxP PxPch *60* K-K3 ....

Not *60* KxP?? B-Q4ch.

60 .... B-Q4

An entirely different situation has now arisen in which both the Rook's capacity for the offensive and the compensating power of Black's passed Pawn have been heightened. The Pawn, moreover, is guarded by Bishops stationed at secure strongholds.

61 B-B1 ....

Of course not *61* BxB, PxB. With two passed connected Pawns for the Exchange, Black has no danger of losing.

61 .... K-B1 *62* R-R7! ....

For the Rook, the promised land: the seventh rank.

| 62 .... | B-QB6 | 63 B-R3 | B-N5 |

The Black Bishop returns because, after the plausible 63 ... B-Q5ch; 64 K-K2, P-B6, White wins a Pawn by 65 R-QB7.

| | 64 B-N2 | K-N1 |

Perhaps here one might expect 64 ... P-B6. Black rightly omits this advance since his King Bishop then loses its mobility. It cannot then, among other things—as happens in the game —come to the rescue via B6 to counteract White's King-side operations.

| | 65 R-Q7 | .... |

White prepares the decisive breakthrough, P-B5.

| 65 .... | B-B3 | 66 R-Q6 | .... |

Here he forces the Bishop back.

| 66 .... | B-Q4 | 67 R-Q8ch | K-B2 |
| | | 68 R-Q7ch | K-N1 |

With an eye toward things to come, Black's King prefers to avoid the black squares. Note also 68 ... K-K1 fails against 69 R-KN7.

| | 69 B-B1 | .... |

A last preparatory measure. On 69 P-B5 at once there follows 69 ... NPxP; 70 K-B4, B-Q7ch.

| | 69 .... | B-QB6 |

On 69 ... B-B3; 70 R-Q6, White gains a *tempo* by the same method as with moves 66-68. With the text move, Black's King Bishop can at least come to the support of the defense.

| | 70 P-B5! | .... |

A clear demonstration of the power of White's Pawn majority on the right wing. Upon *70 ... NPxP; 71 K-B4*, to be followed by *72 P-N6*, White's King marches in.

| 70 .... | BxP | 71 P-B6 | .... |

Now White has a tremendous passed Pawn. It will sooner or later assert itself.

| 71 .... | B-Q5ch! | 72 K-K2 | B-K5 |
| | | 73 B-R3! | .... |

A subtle threat: *74 P-B7ch, K-N2; 75 P-B8(Q)ch, KxQ; 76 RxB!*

| 73 .... | B-Q6ch | 74 K-Q2 | P-K4 |

By this extra protection of his King's Bishop, Black parries the threat mentioned (which would begin now with 75 P-B7ch).

| 75 R-N7ch | K-R1 | 76 R-Q7 | .... |

A little measure to gain time on the clock.

| 76 .... | K-N1 | 77 R-N7ch | K-R1 |
| | | 78 R-QB7 | P-K5 |

Again an extremely critical situation has come up. The Black passed Pawns may march on on all sides. A single *tempo* can decide the issue.

Just how much the initiative counts is clearly revealed here. Had White not made timely provision for a passed Pawn which carries attendant mating threats, his advantage of the Exchange would have become quite worthless. And he'd be faced now with a grim task of holding back Black's passed Pawns.

79 BxP   ....

White has no choice, but there is no need for one.

79 ....   P-K6ch   80 K-B1!   ....

80 K-K1? B-B6ch! etc.

80 ....   P-K7   81 B-N4   ....

Again, the only move.

81 ....   B-K6ch

On *81* ... P-B6, *82* R-K7, and thereafter *83* P-B7 decides the issue.

| *82* K-N2 | BxP | *83* P-B7 | B-B3ch |

Now Black's move is forced (*83* ... B-R3? *84* B-B3ch, and White queens *with check*).

| *84* K-R3 | B-N2 | *85* B-B3! | .... |

Anyway!

| *85* .... | Resigns |

An end game rich in combinations, but one in which the strategical outlines are clearly defined, too.

BUGABOOS OF "BISHOPS OF OPPOSITES"

The major theme of this remarkably thorough end-game study is White's winning chances against that drawing bugaboo, Bishops of opposite colors. As for the themes subsidiary to this one, Dr. Euwe's own summations, particularly those after the first, second, and fifth diagrams, are so apt and develop so logically with the progress of the game that we feel we do best to refer the reader to them.

Championship of the Netherlands
Amsterdam, 1954
FOUR KNIGHTS' GAME

N. CORTLEVER		J. BARENDREGT	
White		*Black*	
1 P-K4	P-K4	12 PxP	PxP
2 N-KB3	N-KB3	13 Q-K2	P-N3
3 N-B3	N-B3	14 QxP	QxQ
4 P-Q4	PxP	15 RxQch	K-Q1
5 NxP	NxP	16 B-B4	B-QB4
6 QNxN	Q-K2	17 R-Q1	R-K1
7 P-KB3	P-Q4	18 RxRch	KxR
8 B-QN5	B-Q2	19 BxP	B-K3
9 BxN	PxB	20 P-QN3	R-B1
10 O-O	PxN	21 B-Q6	BxNch
11 R-K1	P-KB4	22 RxB	P-B4

Bishops of opposite color, but at least the Rooks are still on the board, and so the winning chances for the stronger side are considerably enhanced. Expressed in numbers, the winning-drawing proportion is 3 to 7; but with the Rooks, the ratio is exactly reversed.

Other characteristics that favor the stronger side are:

(1) Freedom of movement for the attacking King, possi-

bilities for invading the hostile position, which applies to the end game in general;

(2) Complications on both wings, especially applicable if not essential when the Bishops of opposite color only are present;

(3) Vulnerability of one or more of the enemy Pawns, which especially is the case in the present end game.

In view of the last point, it is clear that White must prevent the further advance of Black's Bishop Pawn. After 23 R-Q1, P-B5, for instance, a draw soon becomes an accomplished fact. White must therefore force through P-B4 himself. Yet he cannot do this simply by 23 R-KR4, P-KR4; 24 P-B4 because of the surprising 24 ... B-N5! (threatening 25 ... P-N4); 25 B-B4, R-Q1; 26 P-KR3, R-Q8ch; 27 K-R2, B-B4 with all sorts of chances for Black.

Hence there is nothing left but the continuation in the game.

23 R-QR4!   ....

White gains time for blocking Black's Bishop Pawn by the threat on his Queen Rook Pawn.

23 ....   R-B3

Thanks to this *tempo*, Black can save that Rook Pawn.

24 B-B4   P-QR3   25 P-B4   ....

White has realized his first objective. The remarkable thing about his process, however, is that he has done so by incurring what seems to be a most serious handicap: the shut-in condition of his Rook. True, Black can make no serious attempt to capture that Rook. But White, on the other hand, can free it only by the expedient of eliminating Black's Bishop Pawn.

That is the problem which White now faces, and it does not look as though he can solve it in a satisfactory manner. For P-QN4, at one time or another, must cost White his Bishop Pawn, and even the isolation of that Pawn in itself scuttles White's chances of winning. Hence, the only possibility lies in the capture of Black's Bishop Pawn.

To capture that Pawn, White must attack it more often than it can be defended. He can bring about the following setups: White: R on QR5, B on K3; Black: K on Q3, R on QB3; or White: R on QR5, B on KB8; Black: K on QN3, R on QB3. But, in either case, the Black defense is adequate. So White's King must somehow play a role. But how?

Let us, therefore, permit the players first to have their say.

| 25 .... | K-Q2 | 27 B-K3 | K-Q3 |
| 26 R-R5 | B-B4 | 28 K-B2 | P-R4 |

Since in some variations to arise later the unguarded state of Black's KN3 becomes a pertinent factor, it is important to note here that (28) ... P-R4 is unavoidable, in the long run. As soon, in fact, as White's King arrives at KN5, the capture of Black's King Rook Pawn (at R2) is threatened, by K-KR6 in conjunction with B-N5. For Black's King and Rook, both committed to the defense of his Bishop and Queen Rook Pawns, will be unable to aid the defense of the King Rook Pawn. (A vivid demonstration of the import of Characteristic 3 listed after the first diagram.)

| 29 P-N3 | B-N8 | 30 K-K2 | B-B4 |
| | | 31 K-Q2 | B-N5 |

For the time being both engage in a rather pointless bit of wood shifting: probing the terrain. But possibly also diversional maneuvering.

32 K-B3   B-K3

But this Black move thoroughly deters White from any future intent of forcing his Queen Knight Pawn through: his Bishop Pawn falls after 33 P-QN4? PxPch.

33 K-Q3	B-B4ch	35 K-B2	B-B4
34 K-K2	B-N5ch	36 B-B4ch	K-Q2
		37 B-K5?	....

White lifts the pressure on QB5 and by so doing enables Black to undertake a counter-attack which causes his chances for drawing to rise significantly.

37	K-B1	38 B-B4	....

White's Bishop hurriedly resumes its former post but is already too late.

38	K-N2	39 B-K3	K-N3

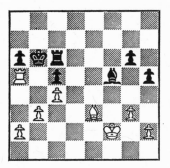

Now *40* RxBP, RxR; *41* P-QN4 does not work because of *41* . . . B-K3. Black then wins the Bishop Pawn and secures a matter-of-fact draw. *40* P-QN4, moreover, is impractical in view of *40* . . . B-Q6, likewise compensating Bishop Pawn for Bishop Pawn. So the White Rook is forced to retreat.

40 R-R3   K-B2?

Time pressure! It is clear, true enough, that *40* . . . P-R4? fails against *41* B-Q2. But Black's text move definitely is not necessary.

He probably feared (*41*) P-QN4, but he can, for the present, prevent that advance with *40* . . . B-Q6. If White thereupon prepares to approach with his King, Black's Rook goes into action: *41* K-K1, R-K3; *42* K-Q2, B-B8, and soon there remains nothing for White but P-QN4, again swapping Pawn for Pawn and bringing the draw much closer.

The text move soon reinstates the former situation: Black's King tied down at Q3; White's free as a bird.

41 P-R4   . . . .

Better is *41* K-K2, to forestall . . . B-Q6, plus . . . K-QN3.

41 . . . .   B-K5   *42* K-K2   . . . .

Now . . . B-Q6 is ruled out, and so, too, . . . K-QN3 (as then White has the resource of P-QN4).

42 . . . .   B-B4   *43* R-R5   K-Q3

43 . . . K-N3 fails against *44* P-QN4, as *44* . . . B-K3 is met by *45* K-Q3.

44 K-B3   . . . .

White could also have reached this position by his thirty-sixth move. So it is evident that the Queen-side intermezzo was entirely superfluous. Meanwhile it is not at all clear as yet just what White aims at with the King's march which follows.

| 44 .... | B-B7 | 45 K-B4 | B-N8 |

Black must stall. He can play the Bishop only.

| 46 P-KN4! | .... |

Ultimately the exchange thus initiated serves to extend the KN-3-Q6 diagonal, whereby White's Bishop can deliver checks at more than one square.

| 46 .... | PxP |

Upon 46 ... B-Q6 there follows 47 K-N5, and Black virtually must submit to 47 ... B-K7; 48 KxP, BxNP (not 48 ... PxP; 49 P-R5! etc.); 49 K-B6 after which the position is much like that after move 51 in the actual game. The sole differences are in the positions of the Bishops, and the reader can readily verify that White can also win in this position after seeing our subsequent comments.

| 47 KxP | B-B4ch | 48 K-N5 | B-N8 |

The crucial position. White's plans assume more substantial patterns: to gain K5 for his King, whereby Black's King will no longer be able to protect its Bishop Pawn.

In its simplest form White's plan is K-B6, B-B4ch, K-K5 and B-K3, winning the Bishop Pawn. For the moment, however, a tactical rejoinder exists: *49* K-B6, K-Q2dis.ch; *50* K-K5, R-K3ch; *51* K-B4, R-K5ch.

From this it is seen that White's Bishop is not posted to advantage as of now. Also, we now sense the reason for White's forty-sixth move—as well as for his next one.

49 B-B2   B-Q6

Now the effectuation of White's plans meets with other objections: *50* K-B6, K-B2dis.ch; *51* K-K5, and White's Bishop Pawn falls if *52* P-N4.

50 B-N1!   . . . .

Nothing more than a *tempo* move. Black's Bishop stands at a crossing: on the one hand, it is important to keep White's Bishop Pawn under attack as just indicated; on the other, the Bishop must guard its Knight Pawn (compare the comments to Black's twenty-eighth move).

50 . . . .   B-N8

Black suffers from a species of *zugzwang*. He cannot give up the Knight Pawn. So he foregoes the attack on White's Bishop Pawn.

51 K-B6!   . . . .

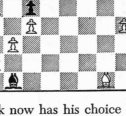

It is all over. Black now has his choice between two losing variations:

(1) *51* . . . K-B2dis.ch; *52* K-K5, K-N3; *53* P-N4! B-Q6; *54* BxPch and *55* K-Q4;

(2) *51* . . . B-Q6 as in the game.

51	B-Q6	52 B-R2ch	. . . .

Here at last the original plan.

52	K-Q2dis.ch	53 K-K5	K-B2

Black realizes that to allow *54* B-N1 plus *55* BxP is altogether hopeless.

54 K-Q5dis.ch   . . . .

A series of discovered checks with the Kings. At this point *54* B-N1, K-N3; *55* P-N4 fails as before since White's Bishop Pawn falls. On the other hand, the continuation chosen would also have been fruitless if Black's Bishop now stood at N8.

54	K-N3	55 RxRPch!	. . . .

The final finesse.

55	. . . .	KxR	57	KxP	BxP
56	KxR	B-N8	58	P-N4	. . . .

White has won and preserved a two-Pawn lead and secures the game with ease.

58	. . . .	K-N2	62	P-B6ch	K-R1
59	P-N5	B-N8	63	K-B5	B-N7
60	K-N4	B-K5	64	P-N6	BxP
61	P-B5	B-B6	65	KxB	P-N4
			66	P-N7ch	Resigns